Brief French Reference Grammar

Roman Colbert
SANTA MONICA COLLEGE

D. VAN NOSTRAND COMPANY

New York Cincinnati Toronto London Melbourne

D. Van Nostrand Company Regional Offices:
New York   Cincinnati

D. Van Nostrand Company International Offices:
London   Toronto   Melbourne

10   9   8   7   6   5

Preface

This book has been designed to present the basic concepts of French grammar in an easily accessible format. It is intended to serve as a convenient reference handbook and is therefore not exhaustive in treatment. In order to avoid the complexities inherent in very detailed grammar manuals, the author has aimed to provide:

1. A tool for instructors to refer students easily to pertinent grammar problems.
2. A concise but thorough review and reference guide for students.
3. A practical format for quick and easy location of rules and examples.
4. Complete listings of verbs, including those requiring prepositions.
5. Useful lists of cognates and false cognates, idiomatic expressions, and others.
6. A comprehensive index designed to facilitate reference and review.

This book contains no grammar exercises, drills, or translation passages. No attempt has been made to make it conform to the characteristic patterns of a standard review grammar. It is strictly a reference guide enabling the student to learn or review the basic French grammar rules and to master their difficulties.

Contents

1 L'article

Nouns in French are normally preceded by an *article*, unless replaced by a possessive adjective (**mon, ma, son, sa**, etc.), a demonstrative adjective (**ce, cette**, etc.), a cardinal number (**deux, cinq, cent**, etc.), or an expression of quantity (**beaucoup de, trop de**, etc.).

1.1 L'article indéfini   un, une, des

Indefinite articles refer to objects or persons not specifically identified.

MASC.	**un** livre	*a book*	**des** livres	*books*
FEM.	**une** chaise	*a chair*	**des** chaises	*chairs*

1.2 L'article défini   le, la, l', les

MASC.	**le** livre	*the book*	**les** livres	*the books*
FEM.	**la** fenêtre	*the window*	**les** fenêtres	*the windows*

When the following noun begins with a vowel, **le** and **la** become **l'**.

MASC.	**l'**appartement
FEM.	**l'**université

A. **L'article défini** indicates a definite thing or person.

MASC.	**le livre du professeur**
FEM.	**la classe de français**

B. It is used to designate a general class, an entire category of persons or things, or a general concept. In this case it is normally omitted in English.

L'argent est nécessaire.	*Money is necessary.*
Les livres sont utiles.	*Books are useful.*
J'aime **les chiens**.	*I like dogs.*

The definite article is required:

C. In front of geographical names, with the exception of cities.

Paris est la capitale de **la France**.

les États-Unis	**la Californie**
le Potomac	**le Mont Everest**

D. Before names of languages except after **en** and **parler.**

> **L'espagnol** est facile.
> Il me dit **en anglais** qu'il **parle français.**

E. Giving dates.

> **le 15 septembre 1971**

F. With the name of the day of the week to express regular recurrence or referring to a particular day.

> Je vais à l'église **le dimanche.**
> **le samedi** suivant

1.3 Les articles contractés   **du, des, au, aux**

When the preposition **de** or **à** precedes the article **le** or **les**, they contract.

de + le = du	**de + les = des**
à + le = au	**à + les = aux**

des (contracted article) meaning *of the* or *from the* should not be confused with **des** (indefinite article, plural of **un** or **une**).

1.4 Les articles partitifs   **du, de la, de l'**

In addition to meaning *of the* or *from the*, these articles may also indicate an unspecified quantity. This meaning is expressed in English by *some* or *any* and is often only implied.

Prenez-vous **du sucre?**	*Do you take sugar?*
Donnez-moi **de l'argent.**	*Give me some money.*
Je mange **de la viande.**	*I eat meat.*
Avez-vous **de la place?**	*Do you have any room?*

Le sucre, la viande, l'argent, le café, le vin, l'eau, le jus, l'imagination, l'intelligence, la chance, etc., represent things that are not composed of easily countable units. Unspecified quantity is therefore expressed in French by the **article partitif**, formed by placing **de** in front of the whole category.

de + la viande	Je désire **de la viande.**
de + la chance	J'ai **de la chance.**
de + l'argent	Je veux **de l'argent.**
de + le sucre	Je prends **du sucre.**

Most nouns are easily countable: **livres, fenêtres, amis, fruits.** The article **des** is then used.

> Nous avons **des examens.**
> J'achète **des fruits.**
> Je mange **des légumes.**

2   L'élision

A. The mute **e** of two-letter words is dropped before words beginning with a vowel and is replaced by an apostrophe.

Je + ai becomes j'ai.
Je ne + ai pas becomes je n'ai pas.

Following this rule: **je, me, te, de, ne, se, le**

B. The **a** of **la** (article or pronoun) is also elided.

l'université	l'étudiante	l'imagination
J'aime Alice.	Je l'aime.	

C. The **e** of **que** and most compounds of **que** is elided.

Qu'avez-vous?
Faites ce **qu'il** vous demande.
Parce **qu'il** fait beau.

D. The **i** of **si** is dropped before **ils** and **il** only.

S'il travaille, il réussira.
S'ils partent à temps, ils arriveront à l'heure.

E. Elision occurs before nouns beginning with mute **h**.

l'homme	l'habitude

F. No elision (or liaison) before aspirate **h**.

le héro	les héros	la honte

G. No elision (or liaison) before **onze** and **huit**.

le onze septembre	le huit février

H. List of the most important words beginning with aspirate **h**.

la hache	le haillon	haïr
la haie	le hamac	haleter
la haine	le hameau	hanter
la halte	le hangar	harasser
la hanche	le harem	harceler
la harpe	le hareng	hérisser
la hâte	le haricot	heurter
la hausse	le harnais	hisser
la hernie	le harpon	hocher
la hiérarchie	le hasard	humer
la honte	le hérisson	hurler
La Hollande	le héron	hagard
la houille	le héros	hardi
la housse	le heurt	haut
la hideur	le hibou	hors
la hutte	le hublot	huit

3 La forme interrogative

Any statement may be converted into a question by placing **est-ce que** in front of it. It has no English equivalent. It is merely a device to introduce a question.

Robert a fini son travail.   **Est-ce que** Robert a fini son travail?
Elle a une robe bleue.   **Est-ce qu'**elle a une robe bleue?

3.1 La forme interrogative avec inversion

A. Pronoun subject.

A question is introduced by putting the subject pronoun after the verb.

Vous avez un stylo.   **Avez-vous** un stylo?

B. Noun subject.

If the subject of the verb is a noun, do not change the order of the sentence; add the appropriate subject pronoun *after* the verb.

Alice est malade.
Alice est-elle malade?

Les jeunes filles sont au cinéma.
Les jeunes filles sont-elles au cinéma?

C. A **t** must be inserted in the third person singular form when the verb ends in a vowel.

Il va.   **Va-t-il?**
Elle parle.   **Parle-t-elle?**
On mange.   **Mange-t-on?**
Il y a une université.   Y **a-t-il** une université?

D. The inversion of **je** is avoided, except with a few verbs.

Suis-je?   **Puis-je?**   **Ai-je?**   **Devrais-je?**

3.2   Est-ce que

Use **est-ce que** for the first person singular.

> **Est-ce que je prononce** bien?   **Est-ce que je sors** avec vous?

If additional information is sought, the following interrogative words can be placed in front of **est-ce que** or the sentence with inversion.

quand	*when*	**où**	*where*
comment	*how*	**qui**	*who*
combien de	*how many*	**que** or **qu'**	*what*
pourquoi	*why*		

> **Quand est-ce que** nous sortons?   **Où** allez-vous?
> **Qu'est-ce que** vous voulez?   **Combien de livres** a-t-il?

4 La forme négative: ne ... pas

Sentences are made negative by placing **ne** or **n'** before the verb and **pas** after it.

Je parle.   Je **ne** parle **pas**.
Elle est au restaurant.   Elle **n'**est **pas** au restaurant.

4.1 In a compound tense, the past participle is placed after **pas**.

Nous **ne** sommes **pas** arrivés.   Il **n'**a **pas** mangé.

4.2 The object pronouns are always placed between **ne** and the verb.

Je ne **le lui** donne pas.   Il ne **les leur** a pas donnés.
Il n'y a pas de nuages.   Ne **les** avez-vous pas vus?

4.3 In an interrogative negative sentence, **pas** is placed after the subject pronoun.

N'entrent-ils **pas**?   N'est-ce **pas**?   N'en prend-elle **pas**?

4.4 Ne is common to all negations, but special negative meanings may be obtained by replacing **pas** by other negative particles.

ne ... point	same meaning as **ne ... pas** but more literary.
ne ... guère	*hardly, scarcely* (Elle n'a **guère** parlé.)
ne ... jamais	*never* (Il **ne** va **jamais** au cinéma.)
ne ... rien	*nothing* (on ne m'a **rien** dit.)
ne ... personne	*nobody* (Je **ne** vois **personne**.)
ne ... plus	*no longer, not any more* (Il **ne** fume **plus**.)
ne ... aucun (nul)	*none, not any* (Il n'y a **aucun** danger.)
ne ... ni ... ni	*neither ... nor* (Elle **n'**a **ni** amis **ni** argent.)
ne ... que	*only* (Il **n'**a **que** des ennuis.)

In a compound tense, **que** is placed after the past participle.

Ils ne m'ont donné **que** des conseils.

The same rule applies to **personne, aucun, nul, ni ... ni**.

[8]

A. The negatives **rien** and **personne** may serve as subjects. In that case they stand first in the sentence.

Rien ne l'intéresse.   **Personne n'**y est allé.

The same rule applies to **ne . . . ni . . . ni, ne . . . aucun (nul)**.

> **Ni** Alice **ni** Robert **ne** sont venus.
> **Ni** lui **ni** son ami **n'**est ici.
> **Aucun** travail **n'**est trop difficile.

B. Two or more negative words (but not **pas**) may be used at one time.

> Alice **ne** voit **plus jamais personne.**
> *Alice never sees anybody anymore.*

When in combination, the order is: (1) **plus**; (2) **jamais**; (3) **rien**; (4) **personne**.

4.5 In front of an infinitive, **ne** and **pas** stay together.

> Il est difficile de **ne pas** parler.

The same rule applies to **plus, jamais,** and **rien**.

> Je leur ai demandé de **ne jamais** sortir seules.
> Il est facile de **ne rien** faire.
> J'ai décidé de **ne plus** travailler le soir.

4.6 The negative expressions and their corresponding affirmatives.

ne . . . jamais	**quelquefois**	**souvent**	**toujours**
never, not ever	*sometimes*	*often*	*always*
ne . . . plus	**encore**		
not any more	*still*		
ne . . . pas encore	**déjà**		
not yet	*already, yet*		
ne . . . personne	**quelqu'un**	**tout le monde**	
nobody, not anybody	*somebody, someone*	*everybody*	
ne . . . rien	**quelque chose**	**tout**	
nothing, not anything	*something*	*everything*	

4.7 After a negative verb, the **articles partitifs (du, de la, de l')** become **de** or **d'**.

> Je prends **du** café.   Je ne prends pas **de** café.
> Il a **de l'**argent.   Il n'a pas **d'**argent.
> Ils mangent **de la** viande.   Ils ne mangent pas **de** viande.

un, une, des become **de** after most negative verbs, always after **avoir** and **il n'y a pas,** but *never* after **être.**

Ils ont **une** maison.	Ils n'ont pas **de** maison.
Elles ont pris **un** autobus.	Elles n'ont pas pris **d'**autobus.
Charles a acheté **des** fruits.	Charles n'a pas acheté **de** fruits.

4.8 **Pas** is not used without **ne** except to negate a single word or part of a sentence *not containing a verb.*

Pas de classes!	**Pas d'étudiants!**	**Pas de professeurs!**
Pas aujourd'hui!	**Pas demain!**	**Pas encore!**

5 Liaisons interdites *(prohibited)*

A. Before aspirate **h.**

        un / héros   **des / haches**

B. Before and after **et.**

        Ils sont **voisins / et / amis.**

C. Before **oui** and **onze** (except: Il est onze heures.)

        Mais / oui!   quatre-**vingt / onze**

D. Between a singular noun and an adjective.

        un **enfant / intelligent**   un **étudiant / américain**

6 Les adjectifs

In French, as in English, there are various kinds of adjectives: **qualificatifs** (*qualifying*), **possessifs** (*possessive*), **interrogatifs, démonstratifs, numéraux** (*numeral*), and **indéfinis** (*indefinite*). In French the adjectives vary in gender and in number and must agree with the noun they qualify.

6.1 L'adjectif qualificatif

A. An adjective must be of the same gender and number as the noun or pronoun that it modifies.

un livre important	**des** livres importants
une leçon importante	**des** leçons importantes

B. Feminine of adjectives.

As a general rule, the feminine is formed by adding **e** to the masculine form.

grand	grand**e**	américain	américain**e**
blond	blond**e**	présent	présent**e**

Adjectives used as predicate adjectives (placed after a form of **être** or the equivalent) must agree with the subject in gender and in number.

Le livre est ouvert.	**La** porte est ouverte.
L'oiseau est joli.	**Les** voitures sont jolies.

When a past participle is used as an adjective, it follows the same rule.

un bâtiment bien construit	**des** maisons bien construites
Le cahier est fermé.	**Les** fenêtres sont fermées.

C. Exceptions in irregular feminine forms.

1. If the masculine form already ends with an **e**, it is invariable.

MASCULINE	FEMININE
un homme **malade**	une femme **malade**
un homme **faible**	une femme **faible**

un bâtiment **moderne**	une maison **moderne**
un livre **jaune**	une robe **jaune**
un livre **rouge**	une robe **rouge**
un exercice **facile**	une leçon **facile**

2. Some adjectives double their consonant and add **e**.

MASCULINE	FEMININE	MASCULINE	FEMININE
bon	**bonne**	gros	**grosse**
cruel	**cruelle**	bas	**basse**
ancien	**ancienne**	net	**nette**

3. Some have an irregular form, but they all end with an **e**.

MASCULINE	FEMININE	MASCULINE	FEMININE
faux	**fausse**	favori	**favorite**
complet	**complète**	frais	**fraîche**
discret	**discrète**	inquiet	**inquiète**
vif	**vive**	actif	**active**
long	**longue**	blanc	**blanche**
public	**publique**	sec	**sèche**
doux	**douce**	roux	**rousse**
cher	**chère**	léger	**légère**
premier	**première**	dernier	**dernière**
heureux	**heureuse**	joyeux	**joyeuse**

4. Some adjectives have alternate masculine forms before masculine singular nouns beginning with a vowel. They form the feminine by doubling the last consonant and adding **e**.

un **beau** garçon	un **bel** homme	une **belle** fille
un **nouveau** cinéma	un **nouvel** ami	une **nouvelle** auto
un **vieux** château	un **vieil** édifice	une **vieille** église
un succès **fou**	un **fol** espoir	une **folle** dépense

D. Plural of adjectives

Generally, the plural of masculine and feminine adjectives is formed by the addition of **s**.

un livre intéressant	**des** livres intéressants
la bonne étudiante	**les** bonnes étudiantes

1. Adjectives ending in -s or -x remain unchanged.

le livre épais	les livres épais
l'homme heureux	les hommes heureux
l'air frais	les fruits frais

2. Adjectives ending in **-eau** take an **x** in the plural.

beau	beaux	nouveau	nouveaux

3. Adjectives ending in **-al** change to **-aux**.

cordial	cordi**aux**	légal	lég**aux**
égal	ég**aux**	loyal	loy**aux**
Exceptions: final	finals	fatal	fatals

E. Positions of adjectives.

In French, adjectives usually follow the noun they modify.

un stylo **noir**	un homme **sympathique**	une pelouse **verte**
une robe **bleue**	une chaise **confortable**	le vin **blanc**

A few common adjectives normally precede the noun.

un **beau** tableau	une **bonne** réponse	un **grand** magasin
un **joli** chapeau	une **mauvaise** note	une **petite** auto
un **vieux** monsieur	le **premier** amour	un **long** voyage
une **jeune** fille	la **dernière** place	un **gros** livre

When two adjectives are to be used with a single noun, normal order is followed.

un **grand et beau** tableau   une **belle** robe **blanche**

A few adjectives have two different meanings according to whether they precede or follow the noun.

un **ancien** élève	*a former student*
l'histoire **ancienne**	*ancient History*
un **brave** homme	*a good man*
un homme **brave**	*a brave man*
un **certain** danger	*some danger*
un danger **certain**	*a positive danger*
cher ami	*dear friend*
un chapeau **cher**	*an expensive hat*
un **grand** homme	*a great man*
un homme **grand**	*a tall man*

des **grandes** personnes	*adults*
des personnes **grandes**	*tall people*

Ils habitent la **même** rue.	*They live in the same street.*
la rue **même** de l'accident	*the very street of the accident*

Pauvre fille!	*Poor girl!*
une fille **pauvre**	*a moneyless girl, a poor girl*

ma **propre** chemise	*my own shirt*
ma chemise **propre**	*my clean shirt*

une **seule** femme	*only one woman*
une femme **seule**	*a lonely woman, a woman alone*

une **vraie** catastrophe	*a real catastrophe*
une histoire **vraie**	*a true story*

6.2 L'adjectif possessif

In French, the possessive adjectives agree in gender and number with the possessed object, but their forms are also determined by the possessor. The possessive adjectives in French always *precede* the noun.

j'ai	**mon** stylo	**ma** chaise	**mes** stylos **mes** chaises
tu as	**ton** stylo	**ta** chaise	**tes** stylos **tes** chaises
il a	**son** stylo	**sa** chaise	**ses** stylos **ses** chaises
elle a	**son** stylo	**sa** chaise	**ses** stylos **ses** chaises
nous avons	**notre** stylo	**notre** chaise	**nos** stylos **nos** chaises
vous avez	**votre** stylo	**votre** chaise	**vos** stylos **vos** chaises
ils ont	**leur** stylo	**leur** chaise	**leurs** stylos **leurs** chaises
elles ont	**leur** stylo	**leur** chaise	**leurs** stylos **leurs** chaises

Before feminine nouns beginning with a vowel or mute **h**, the masculine form of the possessive is used.

> **mon** adresse   **ton** enveloppe   **son** amie

6.3 L'adjectif interrogatif   **quel, quels, quelle, quelles**

There is only one interrogative adjective in French which takes various forms according to the gender and number of the nouns it modifies.

> **Quel** sport préférez-vous?
> **Quelle** heure est-il?
> **Quels** journaux lisez-vous?
> **Quelles** langues apprenez-vous?
> De **quelle** couleur est votre voiture?
> Dans **quel** pays habitez-vous?

6.4 L'adjectif démonstratif   **ce, cet, cette, ces**

Demonstrative adjectives point out objects, and they vary according to the gender and number of the objects they point out. Use **ce** before a masculine singular noun beginning with a consonant.

> **Ce** restaurant est mauvais.   **Ce** jardin est beau.

Use **cet** before a masculine singular noun beginning with a vowel or mute **h**.

> **Cet** appartement est agréable.

Use **cette** before any feminine singular noun.

> **Cette** belle rose est rouge.

Use **ces** before any plural noun.

> **Ces** murs sont gris.
> **Ces** chemises sont neuves.

6.5 Les adjectifs numéraux

A. Cardinal numbers.

1	un, une	6	six
2	deux	7	sept
3	trois	8	huit
4	quatre	9	neuf
5	cinq	10	dix

11	onze	82	quatre-vingt-deux etc...
12	douze	90	quatre-vingt-dix
13	treize	91	quatre-vingt-onze
14	quatorze	92	quatre-vingt-douze etc...
15	quinze	100	cent
16	seize	101	cent un
17	dix-sept	102	cent deux etc...
18	dix-huit	200	deux cents
19	dix-neuf	201	deux cent un
20	vingt	202	deux cent deux etc...
21	vingt et un	1000	mille
22	vingt-deux etc...	1001	mille un etc...
30	trente	1100	mille cent, onze cents
31	trente et un	1200	mille deux cents, douze cents
32	trente-deux etc...	1300	mille trois cents, treize cents
40	quarante	1400	mille quatre cents, quatorze cents
41	quarante et un	1500	mille cinq cents, quinze cents
42	quarante-deux etc...	1600	mille six cents, seize cents
50	cinquante	1700	mille sept cents, dix-sept cents
51	cinquante et un	1800	mille huit cents, dix-huit cents
52	cinquante-deux etc...	1900	mille neuf cents, dix-neuf cents
60	soixante	2000	deux mille
61	soixante et un	2001	deux mille un etc...
62	soixante-deux etc...	2100	deux mille cent etc...
70	soixante-dix	10.000	dix mille
71	soixante et onze	100.000	cent mille
72	soixante-douze etc...	1.000.000	un million de...
80	quatre-vingts	2.000.000	deux millions de...
81	quatre-vingt-un	1.000.000.000	un milliard de...

Vingt and **cent** take the **s** of the plural when a number which multiplies them precedes and no other number follows.

quatre-**vingts**	but:	quatre-**vingt**-cinq
trois **cents**	but:	deux **cent vingt**-huit

Mille is invariable.

B. Ordinal numbers.

Ordinal numbers are formed by adding **-ième** to the cardinal number, except **premier**.

deuxième	*second*
troisième	*third*
vingt et unième	*twenty-first*

No article is used if a cardinal number stands before a noun.

trois tables   **six** chaises   **soixante** ans

The article is used with an ordinal number.

le vingtième siècle

C. Fractions.

1/2	un demi, une demie		1/4	un quart
1/3	un tiers		2/3	deux tiers
3/10	trois dixièmes		3/4	trois quarts

6.6 L'adjectif indéfini

Some adjectives in this category are used as adjectives only; others are used as adjectives and pronouns (see **Pronoms indéfinis**).

A. Adjective only.

1. **chaque** (*each*) is used only before a single noun; it is invariable.

> **Chaque raison** a sa valeur.
> Il s'interrompt à **chaque instant.**

2. **quelque(s)** (*some, a few*).

> Cet artiste a **quelque talent.**
> Cette œuvre a **quelque valeur.**
> Il y a **quelques arbres** dans ce jardin.

3. **quelconque(s)** (*any, just any, whatever, mediocre*) generally follows the noun.

> J. P. Sartre n'est pas **un auteur quelconque.**
> Racontez-lui **une histoire quelconque.**
> Ce sont **des films quelconques.**

4. **divers(e)(s)** (*various*) and **différent(e)(s)**

> Le professeur a donné **divers sujets** de compositions.
> **Diverses personnes** se sont présentées.
> Il a discuté **différents projets.**
> **Différentes personnalités** y étaient réunies.

B. Both adjective and pronoun.

1. **aucun(e)** (*no, no one*) and **nul(le)** (*no, none*) are used with **ne** (see **Négation**).

> **Aucun** travail n'est trop difficile.
> Je **ne** connais **aucune** artiste de cinéma.
> **Nul** espoir n'est permis.

2. **autre(s)** (*other*) is placed before the noun.

> Je préfère une **autre voiture**.
> Nous avons d'**autres choses** à faire.

3. **plusieurs** (*several*) is invariable.

> Je connais **plusieurs pays**.
> **Plusieurs réponses** sont possibles.
> Il lui a écrit **plusieurs fois**.

4. **certain(e)(s)** (*some, certain*) is placed before the noun.

> **Certains professeurs** sont injustes.
> **Certaines questions** sont faciles.

If placed after the noun, **certain** is an **adjectif qualificatif** meaning *sure*.

> C'est **un fait certain**.
> **une victoire certaine**

5. **tel(le)(s)** (*such, such as*).

> **tel père, tel fils**
> **Telles** étaient les explications.
> Il faut prendre les femmes **telles** qu'elles sont.
> Ils en ont fait une **telle** histoire!

6. **tout, toute, tous, toutes** (*all, each, every, the entire*).

> Il nous a expliqué **toute la lecture**.
> **Tout danger** est écarté.
> **Tous les hommes** sont mortels.
> **Toutes les raisons** sont bonnes.
> **tous les jours**

Idiomatic:	**tout le monde**	*everybody*
	tous les deux	*both* m.
	toutes les deux	*both* f.

7 L'adverbe

The adverb is invariable and, as its name indicates, usually modifies a verb. It is also used occasionally to modify an adjective or another adverb. Adverbs of quantity may also be used to modify nouns; when so used, the preposition **de** or **d'** is placed before the noun and no article is used.

7.1 Formation of adverbs

A. By adding **-ment** to adjective ending in a vowel.

facile	facile**ment**	absolu	absolu**ment**
poli	poli**ment**	difficile	difficile**ment**
joli	joli**ment**	confortable	confortable**ment**

B. By adding **-ment** to the feminine of adjectives.

grand	**grandement**	précieux	**précieusement**
doux	**doucement**	actif	**activement**
franc	**franchement**	léger	**légèrement**

C. By replacing the endings **-ant** and **-ent** of the masculine adjectives with **-amment** and **-emment**, respectively.

puissant	**puissamment**	méchant	**méchamment**
constant	**constamment**	indépendant	**indépendamment**
évident	**évidemment**	intelligent	**intelligemment**
prudent	**prudemment**	décent	**décemment**

D. Exceptions:

présent	présen**tement**	lent	lente**ment**
commode	commod**ément**	aveugle	aveugl**ément**
confus	confus**ément**	exprès	express**ément**
gentil	genti**ment**	bref	**brièvement**
bon	**bien**	mauvais	**mal**

[20]

7.2 Positions of adverbs

General rule: In simple tenses, the adverb *follows* the verb it modifies.

Elle ne va **jamais** au cinéma.
Nous mangeons **beaucoup**.
Le temps passe **lentement**.

Ils parlent **bien**.
Cette femme voit **mal**.
L'avion arrive **déjà**.

In compound tenses, the adverb *precedes* the past participle.

Elle n'est **jamais** allée au cinéma.
Nous n'avons pas **beaucoup** mangé.

Ils ont **bien** parlé.
Cette femme a **mal** vu.

A. Adverbs of time, such as **hier, aujourd'hui, demain, tard**, and place, such as **ici, là, là-bas, ailleurs**, as well as long adverbs in **-ment**, *follow* the past participle.

On l'a envoyé **là-bas** sans argent.
Le temps a passé **lentement**.
Je lui ai parlé **longuement**.

Ils sont partis **hier**.
Il est arrivé **tard**.
Tu l'as cherché **partout**.

B. Adverbs modifying adjectives or other adverbs always precede the adjective or adverb they modify.

Elle a **extrémement bien** parlé.
Vous êtes arrivé **trop tôt**.

Il m'a **assez bien** reçu.
Il est **très intelligent**.

C. The adverbs of time **toujours, souvent, déjà**, and **jamais** are generally placed before the past participle.

Tu as **toujours** pensé aux autres.
Je n'ai **jamais** fait de ski.

Il lui a **souvent** écrit.
L'avion est **déjà** arrivé.

D. Adverbs such as **beaucoup, trop, assez, bien, mieux, mal, déjà, encore, tant, plus, jamais, aussi** regularly precede the infinitive.

J'aime **assez** aller à la plage.
Il doit **tant** travailler!
Je voudrais **aussi** connaître cette personne.

Il vaut **mieux** voyager.
Il ne faut pas **mal** penser.
On ne doit pas **trop** demander.

E. Expressions of quantity formed with adverbs.

J'ai **assez d'**ennuis!
J'ai **assez d'**imagination.

I have enough troubles!
I have enough imagination.

Il a **tant de** livres!
Il a **tant de** travail!

He has so many books!
He has so much work!

Elle a **peu d'**amis.	*She has few friends.*
Ella a **peu d'**argent.	*She has little money.*
Il a **trop d'**examens.	*He has too many exams.*
Il a **trop d'**ambition.	*He has too much ambition.*
Il y a **beaucoup de** monuments à Paris.	*There are many monuments in Paris.*
Ce peintre a **beaucoup de** talent.	*This painter has much talent.*
J'ai mangé **tant de** fruits!	*I ate so many fruits!*
J'ai bu **tant de** vin!	*I drank so much wine!*
On a **tellement de** problèmes!	*We have so many problems!*
Il a **tellement de** patience!	*He has so much patience!*

F. The adverbs **plus que, moins que, autant que** and the expressions **plus de . . . que, moins de . . . que, autant de . . . que** are used in comparisons (see **Le comparatif**).

G. When **bien de** and **la plupart de** are used to modify a noun, the definite article is used unless replaced by a possessive or demonstrative adjective.

> Il dort **la plupart du temps.**
> *He sleeps most of the time.*
> **La plupart de mes livres** sont neufs.
> *Most of my books are new.*
> **La plupart de ces femmes** sont jolies.
> *Most of these women are pretty.*
> **Bien de ses amis** sont morts.
> *Many of his friends are dead.*

8 Expressions de quantité

As with the expressions of quantity formed with adverbs (except **la plupart de** and **bien de**), no article is used between the preposition **de** and the noun that follows.

une tasse de café	**un morceau de** gâteau
une goutte d'eau	**un amas de** pierres
une poignée de sel	**un verre de** vin
un bouquet de fleurs	**une bouteille de** bière
une douzaine d'œufs	**une série d'images**
une collection de timbres	**une livre de** pain
une dizaine de dollars	**une centaine de** soldats
une valise de vêtements	**une boîte de** bonbons
une tranche de pain	**une rangée d'arbres**

By adding **-aine** to certain cardinal numbers, expressions of quantity are formed which convey the idea of *about.*

une **huitaine** de	une **dizaine** de	une **douzaine** de
une **quinzaine** de	une **vingtaine** de	une **trentaine** de
une **quarantaine** de	une **cinquantaine** de	une **soixantaine** de
une **centaine** de		

Une douzaine is used as a definite measure of *one dozen.*

The preposition **de** is used after many adjectives in French. In that case, do not use an article before plural nouns.

un jardin **plein de fleurs**	un ciel **couvert de nuages**
des pages **pleines de fautes**	un mur **orné de tableaux**

9 Le comparatif

A. **Plus** . . . **que** (*more . . . than*), **moins** . . . **que** (*less . . . than*), and **aussi** . . . **que** (*as much . . . as*) are used with adjectives or adverbs:

OF SUPERIORITY	**plus**		adjective		
OF INFERIORITY	**moins**	+	or	+	**que**
OF EQUALITY	**aussi**		adverb		

> Alice est **plus belle que** Marie.
> L'avion va **plus vite que** l'auto.
> Mon frère est **moins intelligent que** toi.
> Je vais **moins souvent** au cinéma **que** l'année passée.
> Ma mère est **aussi âgée que** mon père.

Si is often used in a negative sentence for **aussi**.

> Elle n'est pas **si bête que** ça.

B. **Plus de** . . . **que**, **moins de** . . . **que**, and **autant de** . . . **que** are adverbial expressions of quantity used in comparison with nouns:

OF SUPERIORITY	**plus de**				
OF INFERIORITY	**moins de**	+	noun	+	**que**
OF EQUALITY	**autant de**				

> Alice a **plus de travail que** Jacques.
> Elle a **moins d'argent que** lui.
> J'ai **autant d'amis que** vous.

C. **Plus de** and **moins de** are followed by numbers.

> Il y a **plus de vingt** étudiants dans la classe.
> J'ai **plus de cent** dollars en banque.
> J'ai **moins de cinq** dollars en poche.

D. In a comparison, the adjectives **supérieur** and **inférieur** are always followed by the preposition à.

Votre idée est **supérieure à** la mienne.

Cette qualité est **inférieure à** celle que vous avez offerte.

E. The comparatives **moins, plus, aussi,** and **autant** have to be repeated before each adjective or adverb.

Cette maison est **plus grande, plus moderne** et **plus belle** que l'autre.

Ta voiture est **moins chère, moins rapide** et **moins confortable** que la mienne.

F. Irregular comparatives.

meilleur   *better*

Being an adjective, **meilleur** must agree in number and gender.

mieux   *better*   adverb (invariable)

10   Le superlatif

A. **le plus**   **le moins**: There are two kinds of superlatives, superiority and inferiority, and they are formed by placing **le, la,** or **les** in front of **plus** or **moins**.

> Marie est **la plus intelligente.**
> Vos réponses sont **les meilleures.**
> Cette fleur est **la moins belle.**

B. If a complement follows, it must be introduced by **de.**

> Marie est **la plus intelligente de la classe.**
> Vos réponses sont **les meilleures de toutes.**
> Cette fleur est **la moins belle du bouquet.**

C. Irregular superlatives.

le meilleur la meilleure les meilleurs les meilleures	*the best* (adjective)
la mieux le mieux les mieux	*the best* (adverb)

D. After a possessive adjective, the definite article is omitted.

> J'ai déchire **ma plus belle** chemise.
> Il a perdu **son meilleur** ami.
> **Ses plus grands** efforts ont été inutiles.

but:

> **Nos amis les plus chers.**
> **Sa conférence la plus médiocre.**

[26]

E. Notes

1. **de plus en plus** (*more and more*); **de moins en moins** (less and less).

> Elle est **de plus en plus malade.**
> Cet étudiant arrive **de plus en plus tard.**
> Ce cours devient **de moins en moins intéressant.**

2. **plus** + verb, **plus** + verb (*the more . . . , the more . . .*).

> **Plus** je lis, **plus** je comprends.
> **Moins** j'étudie, **moins** j'apprends.

3. Some adjectives have two forms.

mauvais:	**plus mauvais(e)(s)**	**le (la, les) plus mauvais(e)(s)**
	pire(s)	**le (la, les) pire(s)**
petite:	**plus petit(e)(s)**	**le (la, les) plus petit(e)(s)**
	moindre(s)	**le (la, les) moindre(s)**
mal (adverb):	**plus mal**	**le plus mal**
	pis	

Note the expression: **de mal en pis** (*from bad to worse*).

11 Les prépositions

Prepositions are *invariable* and show the relationship between two words in a sentence. After a preposition, a French verb is normally in the infinitive form.

Exceptions: After **en** the present participle follows:

> **en parlant**   **en choisissant**   (See **Le participe présent.**)

After **après** the past infinitive follows:

> **après avoir parlé**   **après être sorti**

PRINCIPAL PREPOSITIONS:

à	*to, at, in*
après	*after*
avant	*before*
avec	*with*
chez	*at the home (place) of*
contre	*against*
dans	*in, inside, into, within*
de	*of, from*
depuis	*since*
derrière	*behind, in back of*
devant	*before, in front of*
dès	*since, from, as early as*
durant	*during*
en	*in*
entre	*between*
envers	*towards*
jusque	*till, until*
malgré	*in spite of*
outre	*beyond*
par	*by, through*
parmi	*among*
pendant	*during*
pour	*for*

[28]

sans	*without*
sauf	*except*
selon	*according to*
sous	*under*
suivant	*according to*
sur	*on, upon*
vers	*toward(s), about*
voici	*here is, here are*
voilà	*there is, there are*

PRINCIPAL PREPOSITIONAL PHRASES

à droite de	*to the right of*
à gauche de	*to the left of*
à côté de	*beside, next to*
à l'extérieur de	*on the outside of*
à l'intérieur de	*inside of*
à l'arrière de	*at the back of*
à l'avant de	*at the front of*
au bout de	*at the end of*
au coin de	*at the corner of*
au milieu de	*in the middle of*
au fond de	*at the bottom of*
au sommet de	*at the top of*
au pied de	*at the foot of*
au-dessus de	*above*
au-dessous de	*beneath*
en face de	*opposite, facing*
en haut de	*at the top of*
en bas de	*at the bottom of*
loin de	*far from*
près de	*near*
d'après	*according to*
grâce à	*thanks to*
jusqu'à	*till, until, up to*
par terre	*on the ground, on the floor*

A. Uses of prepositions with geographical terms

1. In front of cities:
   à is equivalent to *in, to*:

   Je vais à **Paris**.   Je suis à **Paris**.

de is equivalent to *from:*

>Je suis arrivé **de Londres**.   Elle part **de Rome** demain.

2. Before continents and feminine countries (all end in mute e except **le Mexique**):
   en is equivalent to *in* and *to* and **de** to *from*:

Nous allons **en France**.	Nous venons **de Turquie**.
en Angleterre.	**d'Italie**
en Allemagne.	**de Floride**.
en Grèce	**d'Afrique**
en Asie	**de Louisiane**
en Espagne	**d'Amérique**

3. Before masculine countries and states:
   au is equivalent to *in* and *to* and **du** to *from*:

Nous allons **au Pérou**.	Nous venons **du Vénézuela**.
au Brésil.	**du Mexique**.
au Maroc.	**du Liban**.
au Texas.	**du Kansas**.
au Nouveau-Mexique.	**du Japon**.

4. Before plural nouns (feminine or masculine):
   aux is equivalent to *in* or *to* and **des** to *from*:

Nous allons **aux États-Unis**.	Nous venons **des États-Unis**.
aux Antilles.	**des Îles Hawaii**.

5. Exceptions: If the first letter of a masculine country is a vowel, use **en** for *in* and *to* and **d'** for *from*:

Nous allons **en Iran**.	Nous venons **d'Israël**.
en Alaska.	**d'Uruguay**.

B. Uses of key prepositions **à, de, chez, dans, en**

1. **à**   The usual meaning is *to, at, in* (see in the verb section **L'infinitif**):

Il étudie à la bibliothèque.	Je vais au restaurant.
Elle mange à la maison.	Il faut rentrer à minuit.
Nous recevons des cadeaux à Noël.	J'écris à mon amie.
On va à l'église le dimanche.	Elle a une classe à une heure.
Il le donne à sa mère.	On est à table.
Je les ai félicités à la fin du concert.	

   à between two nouns or after a noun and before an infinitive is often used to show the purpose or the nature of the object:

une cuiller à thé	*a teaspoon*
une salle à manger	*a dining room*
une brosse à dents	*a toothbrush*
une pince à linge	*a clothes-pin*
une machine à écrire	*a typewriter*

à often replaces **avec**:

| une tarte **aux** pommes | un gâteau **au** chocolat |
| une machine **à** vapeur | une fille **aux** cheveux blonds. |

à placed after the verb **être** or **appartenir** denotes possession:

Cette voiture appartient à mon père.
Ce chien n'est pas à moi.

à is used in many common expressions without an exact equivalent in English:

| Il va à cheval. | Elle va à pied. |
| à bicyclette. | à motocyclette. |

Il lit à haute voix.	*He reads aloud.*
à voix basse.	*in a low voice.*
au temps de	*in the time of*
à l'heure	*on time*
à temps	*in time*
un objet fait à la main	*a handmade object*
son chapeau à la main	*hat in hand*
Sa voiture est à la main.	*His car is on hand.*

à is used before names of parts of the body:

| J'ai mal à la tête. | Je me suis blessé **au** genou. |
| Il a une cicatrice **au** front. | Il a une alliance **au** doigt. |

2. **de**   The usual meaning is *from* or *of* (see the verb section **L'infinitif**).

de denotes possession:	La voiture **de** Paul est rapide.
authorship:	Un poème **de** Verlaine
origin:	Elle sort **de** la bibliothèque.
partitive:	Je mange **de** la viande le soir.
cause:	Elle est morte **de** chagrin.

de between two nouns denotes material or purpose:

une table **de** marbre	une classe **de** français
un rideau **de** fer	une agence **de** voyage
un numéro **de** téléphone	une voiture **de** sport
un roman **d'**amour	une salle **de** bains

de in expressions of quantity:

une tasse **de** café	un verre **de** vin
un morceau **de** gâteau	une douzaine **d'**oeufs
beaucoup **d'**amis	peu **d'**enfants.

3. **chez** This preposition has no parallel in English, and it conveys different meanings according to the context. **Chez** comes from the latin *casa*, which explains why its original meaning was "in the dwelling of." In modern French, it has acquired the following meanings: *at the house of, at the place of, at the place of business of, in the works of, in the country of, in the group of, in the society of*, etc.

Chez always precedes proper names or nouns and pronouns representing persons:

> Je vous attends **chez** moi.
> Vous devez aller **chez** le dentiste.
> On est bien **chez** soi.
> Elle retourne **chez** ses parents.
> **Chez** les Français on mange bien.
> **Chez** les amants tout plaît, tout est parfait.
> **Chez** les catholiques le mariage est sacré.
> La critique, **chez** Voltaire, est mordante.

4. **dans** The usual meaning is *in* or *inside*; dans is always followed by an article or an adjective (possessive or demonstrative):

> Les papiers sont **dans** l'enveloppe.
> Le stylo est **dans** ma serviette.
> Il y a des fautes **dans** cet examen.
> L'auto est **dans** la rue.
> Elle est **dans** sa chambre.
> Il regarde **dans** l'eau.

Dans with an expression of time indicates the future and is the opposite of **il y a** (*it has been, ago*):

> J'aurai fini **dans une heure.**
> Nous partirons **dans trois jours.**
> J'aurai mon diplôme **dans deux ans.**

Dans after the verb **prendre** conveys the meaning *out of*:

> Nous avons pris l'argent **dans** le tiroir.

5. **en** The usual meaning is *in*; **en** is never used before a noun preceded by a definite article. Exceptions are: **en l'honneur de, en l'absence de**, etc.

En denotes place: **en** France
condition: **en** bonne santé
purpose: **en** vente
time: **en** hiver, **en** mars
manner: **en** colère
matter: **en** bois, **en** cuir

Before an expression of time, it indicates the time required to do or accomplish something:

J'ai fait ce travail **en** deux heures.
Il a lu ce livre **en** une nuit.

En used before a present participle (see the verb section).

12 Useful idiomatic expressions requiring a preposition

(For verbs requiring a preposition see l'infinitif.)

rempli de	*filled with*
couvert de	*covered with*
chargé de	*loaded with*
content de	*happy with*
mécontent de	*displeased with*
heureux de	*happy with*
satisfait de	*satisfied with*
avide de	*eager for*
différent de	*different from*
éloigné de	*distant from*
plein de	*full of*
garni de	*furnished with, fitted with*
orné de	*decorated with*
las de	*weary of*
digne de	*worthy of*
indigne de	*unworthy of*
fou de	*very fond of*
fier de	*proud of*
propre à	*fit for*
intéressé à	*interested in*
sensible à	*sensitive to*
adroit à	*skillful at*
enclin à	*prone to*
antérieur à	*prior to*
adonné à	*addicted to*

12.1 Introduced by à

au cours de	*in the course of*
à partir de	*starting from*
à la fois	*at the same time*
à votre tour	*your turn*

à l'heure	on time
à l'heure du repas	at meal time
à toute heure	at all times
à temps	on time
à tout à l'heure	see you in a short while
à tantôt	see you in a little while
au revoir	good-bye
au plaisir	see you
à l'avenir	in the future
au mois de	in the month of
au printemps	in the spring
au passé	in the past
à droite	to the right
à gauche	to the left
au milieu	in the middle
à côté de	next to
au loin	in the distance
au-dessus	above
au-dessous	below
à l'extérieur	on the outside
à l'intérieur	inside
au coin de	at the corner of
au bord de	at the edge of
au bout de	at the end of
à l'étranger	abroad
au début de	at the beginning of
à la télévision	on television
au soleil	in the sun
à la montagne	in the mountains
à la campagne	in the country
à la page	up to date
à la page dix	on page ten
à la ligne	new paragraph
à court de	short of
au nom de	in the name of
à votre santé!	to your health!
à l'usage de	for the use of
aux dépens de	at the expense of
à mes frais	at my expense
au choix	all at the same price (your choice)
à portée de	within reach of
à quoi bon?	what is the use?

à l'aide de	*with the help of*
à l'envers	*inside-out, the wrong way*
à part	*aside*
à la légère	*not seriously*
à la hâte	*in a hurry*
au hasard	*at random*
à l'inverse de	*as opposed to*
à tout prix	*by any means, at any price*
à la mode	*in style*
à moitié	*halfway*
à fond	*thoroughly*
au fond	*basically*
au contraire	*on the contrary*
à volonté	*at will*
à propos de	*with regard to*
à propos . . .	*by the way . . .*
à tort ou à raison	*right or wrong*
à peu près	*about*
au courant	*informed*
à jour	*up to date (for a ledger)*
à cet égard	*in that respect*
à vrai dire . . .	*to tell you the truth . . .*
au lieu de	*instead of*
à l'insu de quelqu'un	*without someone's knowledge*
à mon avis	*in my opinion*
à cause de	*on account of, because*
à bicyclette	*by bicycle*
à pied	*on foot*
à cheval	*on horseback*
au verso	*on the reverse side*
à tue-tête	*at the top of one's voice*
à tête reposée	*at one's leisure*
à sa tête (en faire . . .)	*to have one's way*
au téléphone	*on the telephone*
au beurre	*in butter*
à travers	*across, through*
à haute voix	*aloud*
à voix basse	*in a low voice*
à merveille	*marvelously*
à bientôt	*see you soon*
à demain	*'til tomorrow*
à l'avant	*in the front*

12.2 Introduced by de

de coutume	*usually*
d'habitude	*usually*
d'ordinaire	*ordinarily*
comme d'habitude	*as usual*
de telle manière que	*in such a way that*
de cette façon	*in this manner*
de même	*likewise*
de parti pris	*deliberately*
de force	*by force*
de tout coeur	*whole-heartedly*
d'accord	*O.K., agreed*
de temps en temps	*from time to time*
de temps à autre	*occasionally*
de tout temps	*at all times*
de toute la journée	*all day long (in negative sentences)*
d'ici à	*from here to, between now and . . .*
d'ici là	*between now and then*
d'ici peu	*before long*
de bonne heure	*early*
de jour en jour	*from day to day*
de nos jours	*nowadays*
de bon appétit (manger)	*heartily (to eat)*
de tous côtés	*from all sides*
de côté (mettre)	*aside (to put)*
de mieux en mieux	*better and better*
de plus en plus	*more and more*
de part et d'autre	*from both sides*
d'autre part	*on the other hand*
de la part de	*on behalf of*
de retour (être)	*to be back*
de nouveau	*again*
d'une façon ou d'une autre	*in one way or another*
de haut en bas	*from top to bottom*
de rigueur	*compulsory, a must*
de plein gré	*of one's own free will*
d'occasion	*second hand*
d'avance	*in advance, beforehand*
de mal en pis	*from bad to worse*
d'après	*according to*
d'ailleurs	*besides, furthermore*

de mémoire	*by heart, from memory*
de supplément	*additional, extra*

12.3 Introduced by en

en vigueur	*in force*
en guerre	*at war*
en paix	*in peace*
en haut	*upstairs*
en bas	*downstairs*
en avance	*in advance*
en avant	*in front, forward*
en retard	*late*
en arrière	*in the rear, behind, backwards*
en vacances	*on vacation*
en congé	*on leave*
en voyage	*on a trip*
en face de	*in front of*
en plein hiver	*in the middle of the winter*
en plein air	*in the open air*
en pleine mer	*on the open sea*
en plein jour	*in broad daylight*
en même temps	*at the same time*
en plein soleil	*in the hot sun*
en route	*on the way*
en automne	*in the fall*
en été	*in the summer*
en hiver	*in the winter*
en auto	*by car*
en bateau	*by boat*
en avion	*by plane*
en train	*by train*
en ami	*as a friend*
en deçà de	*this side of*
en moyenne	*on the average*
en plus	*on top, extra*
en tout	*altogether*
en tout et pour tout . . .	*first and last . . .*
en tout ou en partie	*wholly or partly*
en somme	*in short*
en vogue	*in style*
en aucune façon!	*by no means!*

en vérité	*indeed, truthfully*
en effet	*indeed, in fact*
en fait	*in fact, as a matter of fact*
en dépit de	*in spite of*
en particulier	*privately, in particular*
en train de	*in the process of*
en attendant	*in the meantime*
en réalité	*really, actually*
en vente	*for sale*
en marche	*under way*
en marche (mettre)	*to start (an engine)*
en panne (être)	*breakdown*
en souvenir de	*in memory of*
en chômage	*unemployed*

12.4 Introduced by other prepositions

par terre	*on the ground*
par écrit	*written*
par exemple	*for instance*
par exemple!	*upon my word!*
par hasard	*by accident, by chance*
par paresse	*out of laziness*
par suite de	*in consequence of*
par contre	*on the other hand*
par conséquent	*consequently*
par coeur	*by heart*
par ici	*this way*
par amitié	*out of friendship*
par jour	*per day*
sans exemple	*without parallel*
sans doute	*no doubt, probably*
sans aucun doute	*without a doubt*
sur le fait	*in the act*
sur toute la ligne	*all along the line*
sous clé	*under lock and key*

13 Conjonctions et termes de transition

A conjunction is a word which connects words, phrases, or clauses. The most common subordinating conjunctions are **que** (*that*), **comme** (*as*), and **si** (*if*). The conjunction **que** may not be omitted in French:

> J'espère **que** vous viendrez.
> Robert dit **que** son frère est malade et **qu'**il est chez lui.
> Je dois travailler **comme** tout le monde.
> **Comme** je n'étais pas là, elle en a profité.
> Elle viendra **si** vous le lui demandez.
> **Si** l'un dit oui, l'autre dit non.

(See the verb section for the sequence of tenses with if-clauses.)

A. Expressing time:

quand (*when*)	J'irai en Europe **quand** j'aurai l'argent.
lorsque (*when*)	J'aime la plage **lorsqu'**il fait chaud.
dès que (*as soon as*)	**Dès qu'**il me voyait, il tremblait.
aussitôt que (*as soon as*)	**Aussitôt qu'**il arrivera, il mangera.
depuis que (*since*)	Il pleut **depuis que** je suis là.
pendant que (*while*)	Je l'écoute **pendant qu'**il parle.
après que (*after*)	Ils danseront **après qu'**il sera parti.
à mesure que (*while, as*)	**A mesure que** je reculais, il avançait.
tandis que (*whereas*)	Il s'amuse, **tandis que** nous travaillons.
chaque fois que (*each time that*)	**Chaque fois qu'**il me parle, il demande de l'argent.

Note that **depuis que**, **pendant que**, and **après que** are always followed by a verbal expression, but **depuis** and **pendant** are followed by a noun or an expression of time (see Expressions of time and duration):

> Elle ne parle pas **depuis** son retour.
> Je serai à la bibliothèque **pendant** une heure.

[40]

Après requires the past infinitive (see the verb section), a noun, or an expression of time.

> **Après avoir dîné** nous sommes allés au cinéma.
> Je retourne chez moi **après** ma classe de français.

B. Principal coordinating conjunctions:

et	*and*
avec	*with*
car	*because*
parce que	*because*
de même que	*just as, like*
ainsi que	*just as*
ainsi	*so, thus*
ou	*or*
ou bien	*or else*
soit . . . soit	*either . . . or*
tantôt . . . tantôt	*now . . . now*
donc	*therefore*
par conséquent	*consequently*
partant	*therefore*
c'est pourquoi	*that is why*
aussi	*so*
aussi bien que	*as well as*
puisque	*since, as long as*
mais	*but*
pourtant	*however*
cependant	*however*
néanmoins	*nevertheless*
toutefois	*however, yet*
quand même	*anyway*
et puis	*besides, moreover*
d'ailleurs	*besides, moreover*
au surplus	*besides*
au reste	*besides*
du reste	*moreover, besides*
alors	*then*
or	*now, but*
de plus	*besides, moreover*

1. **Car** and **parce que** are always followed by a verbal expression. If a noun follows use **à cause de**:

> Je ne suis pas allé au cinéma **parce que** j'étais enrhumé.
> Je ne suis pas allé au cinéma **à cause de** mon rhume.

Car is never placed at the beginning of a sentence.

2. Do not confuse **quand** as a conjunction, synonym of **lorsque**, and **quand** as an adverb in interrogative sentences:

> **Quand** partons-nous?   **Depuis quand** êtes-vous là?

In these cases **quand** cannot be replaced by **lorsque**.

C. Transition words:

d'abord	*first*	**ensuite**	*afterwards*
puis	*next*	**alors**	*then*
enfin	*at last*	**bref**	*in short*
finalement	*finally*		

D. All the conjunctions we have mentioned take the indicative mood. Here are a few others:

alors que	*while, all the time when*
maintenant que	*now that*
tant que	*as long as*
attendu que	*whereas, seeing that*
vu que	*whereas, seeing that*
suivant que	*according to whether*
selon que	*according to whether*
si	*whether*

E. The following conjunctions may be followed by the indicative or the subjunctive (see the verb section):

> **de sorte que**
> **en sorte que**
> **de manière que**
> **de façon que**

With the indicative, they mean *in a way* or *in a manner*. With the subjunctive, they mean *so that* or *in such a way that*.

F. The following conjunctions require the subjunctive (see the verb section):

jusqu'à ce que	*until*
en attendant que	*until*
pourvu que	*provided that*
supposé que	*supposing that*
bien que	*although*
quoique	*although*
encore que	*although*
afin que	*in order that, so that*
pour que	*in order that, so that*
au cas que	*in case that*
à condition que	*providing that*
sans que	*unless, without*
nonobstant que	*in spite of*
malgré que	*although*
de peur que	*for fear that*
de crainte que	*for fear that*
à moins que	*unless*
avant que	*before*

The pleonastic **ne** is often used with **de peur que, de crainte que, à moins que,** and **avant que** (see **le ne explétif**).

14   Le ne explétif

There are certain French constructions in which **ne** is pleonastic. In these cases **ne** has no
real meaning and does not make the sentence negative; it is strictly a literary form.

A. The pleonastic **ne** is often found after the following conjunctions, which take
the subjunctive:

> **A moins que** vous **ne** fassiez vos devoirs . . .
> Interrogez-la **avant** qu'elle **ne** s'en aille.
> **De peur** qu'elle **ne** soit malade.
> **De crainte** qu'elle ne se fâche.

B. With expressions of fear:

> **Je crains** qu'il **ne** fasse une faute.
> **J'ai peur** qu'il **ne** se casse une jambe en jouant.

C. In a clause following a comparison:

> Elle est **plus intelligente** qu'elle **ne** paraît.

D. With the verbs **nier** and **douter** used negatively or interrogatively:

> **Vous ne pouvez nier** qu'elle **ne** soit malheureuse.
> **Doutez-vous** qu'ils n'arrivent à la lune?

E. With the verbs **éviter, empêcher, faire attention**, and **prendre garde**:

> **Evitez** qu'ils **ne** vous fassent des ennuis.
> **Faites attention** qu'elle **ne** vous domine.
> **Il faut empêcher que** cette catastrophe n'arrive.

All these sentences would still be correct without **ne explétif**.

15 L'inversion

A. It is found in certain question forms (see **la forme interrogative**).

B. After a direct quotation, the explanatory verb is usually followed by the pronoun subject:

>—Je suis prête, **dit-elle**.
>—Ne sortez pas, **ajouta-t-il**.
>—Votre composition est bonne, me **dit-il**.
>—Je vous aime, **écrit-il**.
>—Cela m'est égal, **répondit-elle**.

The most common explanatory verbs are:

dire	**affirmer**
demander	**annoncer**
se demander	**conseiller**
recommander	**commander**
répondre	**ordonner**
ajouter	**répliquer**
téléphoner	**écrire**
répéter	**penser**
s'exclamer	**faire**

C. Inversion occurs in sentences beginning with certain adverbs.

>**Encore faut-il** qu'il se décide.
>**A peine avait-on** mis pied à terre . . .
>Elle est malade, **aussi décide-t-elle** de rester chez elle.
>**Ainsi** en **avons-nous** décidé.

peut-être	*maybe*	**au moins**	*at least*
toujours	*yet, always*	**du moins**	*at least*
sans doute	*probably*	**rarement**	*seldom*
probablement	*probably*	**de là**	*as a result*
ainsi	*thus*	**aussi**	*therefore*
à peine	*hardly*	**encore**	*yet, still*

16 Le nom—genre et nombre

16.1 Feminine forms of nouns

Some nouns referring to persons or animals have a masculine and a feminine form.

A. An **e** is added for the feminine form:

un ami	une ami**e**	un commerçant	une commerçant**e**
un marchand	une marchand**e**	un étudiant	une étudiant**e**

B. Nouns ending in **n** or **t** double the consonant:

un chien	une chie**nne**	un chat	une cha**tte**
un paysan	une paysa**nne**	un sot	une so**tte**

C. A special ending characterizes some feminine form:

un prince	une prin**cesse**	un danseur	une dans**euse**
un lecteur	une lec**trice**	un flatteur	une flatt**euse**
un acteur	une ac**trice**	un directeur	une direc**trice**

un chanteur has two feminine forms   **une chanteuse**
                                                une cantatrice

D. The masculine and the feminine forms are alike and only the article varies:

un catholique	une catholique
un secrétaire	une secrétaire
un acrobate	une acrobate
un artiste	une artiste
un camarade	une camarade

E. If only one form is used for both genders, the article does not vary, and the words **féminin** or **femelle** are added when necessary.

un professeur	**un professeur féminin**
un perroquet	**un perroquet femelle**
un écrivain	Colette est **un écrivain** célèbre.

F. Some feminine forms are distinct:

compagnon	**compagne**
père	**mère**
frère	**soeur**
neveu	**nièce**
mari	**femme**
homme	**femme**
mâle	**femelle**
héros	**héroïne**
oncle	**tante**
garçon	**fille**
fils	**fille**
cheval	**jument**
coq	**poule**
mouton	**brebis**

16.2 Although there is no rule to determine if a noun is masculine or feminine, the following information should be of some practical value to American students.

A. The following nouns are generally masculine:

Persons of the male sex	Exceptions:	**une victime**
		une personne
		une dupe
		une sentinelle
Metals	Exceptions:	**la fonte**
		la tôle
Days, months, seasons		
Colors		
Trees		
Weights and measures	Exceptions:	**une once**
		une lieue
		une livre

B. Nouns with the following endings are generally masculine:

-age	**le fromage**	Exceptions:	**une image**
			une cage
			une plage
			une page
			la nage
			la rage

-al	le mal	
-ail	le vitrail	
-ard	le renard	
-er	le dîner	une cuiller
	le fer	la mer
-el	le sel	
	le gel	
-eau	le gâteau	la peau
		l'eau
-isme	le communisme	
-ment	le serment	la jument
-oir	le miroir	

C. The following nouns are generally feminine:

Persons of the female sex	
Animals of the female sex	
Arts and sciences	la peinture
	la philosophie
	Exception: le dessin
Countries (ending in e)	la France
	Exception: le Mexique
Continents	l'Amérique
Fruits (in e)	la poire
	la pomme

D. Also nouns ending in:

-ade	une promenade	Exceptions:	un grade
-ace	la glace		un espace
-aille	la paille		
-aine	la plaine		un domaine
-ance	la chance		
-asse	la tasse		
-anse	la danse		
-eille	une merveille		
-eine	une peine		
-ence	la prudence		le silence
-esse	la sagesse		
-ense	la défense		
-tion	une action		un bastion
-ille	la fille		le mille
	la ville		
-ise	la chemise		

E. Some nouns have different meanings according to their gender. Here are a few examples:

le critique	*the critic*	la critique	*criticism*
le guide	*the guide*	la guide	*the rein*
un office	*office, function*	une office	*pantry*
un livre	*a book*	une livre	*a pound*
un manche	*a handle*	une manche	*a sleeve*
un pendule	*a pendulum*	une pendule	*a clock*
un mode	*a mood, manner*	une mode	*fashion*
le vase	*the vase*	la vase	*the mud*
un somme	*a nap*	une somme	*a sum*
un voile	*a veil*	une voile	*a sail*

16.3 Plural of nouns

GENERAL RULE: The plural of a noun is usually formed by adding an s to the singular:

un livre	des livres	une chaise	des chaises
le mur	les murs	l'étudiant	les étudiants

A. Nouns ending in -s, -x, and -z are invariable:

un avis	des avis	un nez	des nez
une noix	des noix	un fils	des fils

B. Nouns ending in -au, -eau, and -eu form the plural in x:

un noyau	des noyaux	un gâteau	des gâteaux
un jeu	des jeux	un neveu	des neveux

Exceptions: un pneu   des pneus   un bleu   des bleus

C. Nouns ending in -al form their plural in -aux:

un cheval	des chevaux	un journal	des journaux

Exceptions:

un récital	des récitals
un festival	des festivals
un régal	des régals
un bal	des bals
un cérémonial	des cérémonials

D. A few nouns in **-ail** form the plural in **-aux**:

le travail	les travaux	un bail	des baux
un vitrail	des vitraux	le corail	les coraux
l'émail	les émaux	un soupirail	des soupiraux

E. Seven nouns ending in **-ou** form the plural in **-x**:

un bijou	des bijoux	un chou	des choux
un pou	des poux	un genou	des genoux
un caillou	des cailloux	un joujou	des joujoux
un hibou	des hiboux		

F. The following are irregulars:

un aieul	des **aieux**
le ciel	les **cieux**
un œil	des **yeux**

The plural **ciels** exists in **ciels de lit** (canopies) and **les ciels d'une peinture**.

The plural **œils** occurs in some compound nouns:

des œils-de-boeuf
des œils-de-chat
des œils-de-perdrix

G. Some nouns are always used in their plural form:

| les **archives** | les **vacances** | les **fiançailles** |
| les **mœurs** | les **ténèbres** | les **funérailles** |

Les gens is always plural; feminine if the adjective precedes and masculine if it follows:

de **bonnes gens**   des **gens malheureux**

17   Cognates and false cognates

17.1 Cognates

A number of French and English words have identical or nearly identical spellings and meanings.

Nouns ending in	-tion	admiration	nation	exposition
		addition	action	émotion
	-age	passage	village	carnage
	-itude	solitude	altitude	aptitude
Adjectives ending in	-able	acceptable	passable	stable
	-ible	visible	flexible	possible
	-al	capital	vital	principal

Other groups of words have dissimilar endings but are easily identifiable.

A. Nouns

-ie usually corresponds to *-y*

théorie	*theory*
industrie	*industry*
géologie	*geology*

-té usually corresponds to *-ty*

faculté	*faculty*
légalité	*legality*
vanité	*vanity*
beauté	*beauty*

-teur usually corresponds to *-tor*

moteur	*motor*
conducteur	*conductor*
docteur	*doctor*

-isme usually corresponds to *-ism*

socialisme	*socialism*
réalisme	*realism*

-iste usually corresponds to *-ist*

fataliste	*fatalist*
dentiste	*dentist*
artiste	*artist*

B. Adverbs

-ment usually corresponds to *-ly*

généralement	*generally*
légalement	*legally*
calmement	*calmly*

C. Adjectives

-eux usually corresponds to **-ous**

anxieux	*anxious*
hideux	*hideous*
curieux	*curious*

-if usually corresponds to *-ive*

décisif	*decisive*
subjectif	*subjective*
instinctif	*instinctive*

-ique usually corresponds to *-ic* or *-ical*

physique	*physical*
fantastique	*fantastic*
dynamique	*dynamic*
électrique	*electrical*

-ant usually corresponds to *-ing*

charmant	*charming*
dominant	*dominating*

The circumflex accent (^) often means that the **s** was dropped:

forêt	*forest*
hôpital	*hospital*
rôti	*roast*

17.2 False Cognates

achever	to complete
actuel	at the present, current
assister	to attend
attendre	to wait
blesser	to wound, to injure
le but	the goal
la cave	the cellar
la chair	the flesh
la chance	the luck
le coin	the corner
crier	to shout
dérober	to steal
la figure	the face
la franchise	the frankness
le front	the forehead
un habit	a suit
une injure	an insult
joli	pretty
large	wide
une lecture	a reading
la librarie	the bookstore
la location	the renting, the booking
le magasin	the store
la monnaie	the small change
or	now, well, gold
une pièce	a room, a play
une place	a seat
quitter	to leave
une rente	a pension
rester	to remain
un roman	a novel
rude	rough
sensible	sensitive
le sort	destiny
sympathique	nice, likable
user	to wear out
la veste	the jacket, the coat

18   Les accents

18.1 é   L'accent **aigu** occurs only over the é:

     été   bébé   thé   fermé   clé

18.2 (`)   L'accent **grave** occurs over the vowel è:

           très   après   père

It also occurs over the vowels à and ù without affecting their sound. It is used to distinguish between two words with identical spellings but different meanings:

à	*to*	où	*where*	là	*there*
a	*have*	ou	*or*	la	*the*

18.3 (^)   L'accent **circonflexe** may occur over any vowel. Over ê it has the same sound as è:

           un **rêve**   une **tête**

It does not affect the sound of the other vowels:

     une **boîte**   un **gîte**   un **hôtel**   la **hâte**   une **flûte**   sûr

19 Nomenclature grammaticale

ADJECTIVE: **l'adjectif**

> a descriptive, qualifying, or limiting word modifying a noun.

ADVERB: **l'adverbe**

> A word which modifies a verb, an adjective, or another adverb.

ANTECEDENT: **l'antécédent**

> The word, phrase, or clause previously mentioned to which a pronoun refers.

APOSTROPHE: **l'apostrophe**

> A sign (') used to show the omission of a letter.

ARTICLE: **l'article**

> The word placed in front of a noun reflecting its gender and indicating if it is definite or indefinite.

AUXILIARY VERB: **le verbe auxiliaire**

> A helping verb by means of which a compound tense is formed (**avoir** and **être**), or by means of which a recent past (**venir de**) or a near future (**aller**) is expressed.

CAPITAL LETTER: **majuscule**

CEDILLA: **cédille (ç)**

CAUSATIVE: **causatif**

> A verb whose subject causes the action to be done by someone else (**faire**): **Se faire laver** les cheveux.

CLAUSE: **proposition**

> Subordinate: **subordonnée**
> Principal: **principale**

> Any group of words containing a subject and a predicate.

COMPOUND TENSE: **temps composé**

A verbal phrase made up of a conjugated auxiliary verb and a past participle of a second verb.

CONJUNCTION: **conjonction**

A word used to link words, phrases, or clauses.

CONDITIONAL: **conditionnel**

CONSONANT: **consonne**

DASH: **tiret**

DEMONSTRATIVE: **démonstratif**

A word which indicates or points out the person or the thing referred to.

DIAERESIS: **tréma**

DIRECT OBJECT: **objet direct**

A noun or pronoun receiving the action of a transitive verb without a preposition: J'aime **les roses**.

DISJUNCTIVE PRONOUN: **pronom accentué ou disjonctif**

A pronoun separated from the verb in the sentence.

ENDING: **la terminaison**

EXPLETIVE: **explétif**

A word not needed for the sense such as **ne explétif**.

GENDER: **le genre**

Masculine or feminine property of nouns and pronouns.

HYPHEN: **trait d'union**

IDIOM: **idiome**

A set expression having a meaning different from the literal or contrary to the usual patterns of the language.

IMPERATIVE: **l'impératif**

The form of the verb that expresses a command or a request.

IMPERFECT: **l'imparfait**

INDICATIVE: **l'indicatif**

INDIRECT OBJECT: **l'objet indirect**

A noun or pronoun receiving the action of a verb through the preposition **à** or **de**.

INFINITIVE: **l'infinitif**

The form of the verb that expresses the general meaning of the verb without regard to person, number, or time.

INTRANSITIVE VERB: **verbe intransitif**

A verb that does not require a direct or an indirect object to complete its meaning.

IRREGULAR VERB: **verbe irrégulier**

A verb which does not follow one of the regular conjugation patterns.

INTERROGATIVE: **l'interrogatif**

A form used for asking a question.

INVERSION: **l'inversion**

Reversal of normal order of subject and verb.

MOOD: **le mode**

The point of view from which the action or statement is seen: factual **(l'indicatif)**, dependent on other conditions **(le conditionnel)**, subjective, wishful, doubtful, possible, fearful **(le subjonctif)**, and commands **(l'impératif)**.

NOUN: **le nom** ou **le substantif**

A word used to name a person, place, or quality.

NUMBER: **le nombre**

singular or plural.

PARTICIPLE: **le participe**

The form of the verb which indicates time but not the person. **Le participe présent** (*present participle*) ends in **-ant** (-ing in English). **Le participe passé** (*past participle*) is the form used, together with the auxiliary verb, to form all compound tenses.

PARTITIVE: **le partitif**

A construction (**de** + definite article) indicating a part of a whole or an indefinite quantity.

PARENTHESIS: **la parenthèse**

PREDICATE: **l'attribut**

PREPOSITION: **la préposition**

A word placed before a noun or pronoun to show its relationship to some other word in the sentence.

PLUPERFECT: **le plus-que-parfait**

PRONOUN: **le pronom**

A word used in place of a noun and often replacing a group of words or a whole idea.

PUNCTUATION: **la ponctuation**

QUESTION MARK: **le point d'interrogation**

QUOTATION MARKS: **les guillemets**

REFLEXIVE VERB: **le verbe pronominal** ou **réfléchi**

A verb expressing an action in which the subject and the recipient of the action are the same.

RELATIVE PRONOUN: **le pronom relatif**

A pronoun which joins two clauses, the antecedent being in the main clause.

SEMICOLON: **le point-virgule**

SMALL LETTER: **une minuscule**

SUBJECT: **le sujet**

The word denoting the person or thing that performs the action (active voice) or that receives the action (passive).

STEM: **le radical**

SUBJUNCTIVE: **le subjonctif** (see MOOD)

TENSE: **le temps**

The form of the verb expressing the time of the action.

VERB: **le verbe**

A word which expresses an action or a state of being.

VOICE: **la voix**

> **la voix active**: if the subject acts (active).
> **la voix passive**: if acted upon (passive).

20 Les pronoms

In French, as in English, there are various kinds of pronouns: **les pronoms personnels** (*personal*), **les pronoms possessifs** (*possessive*), **les pronoms démonstratifs** (*demonstrative*), **les pronoms relatifs** (*relative*), **les pronoms indéfinis** (*indefinite pronouns*), and **les pronoms interrogatifs**.

The pronoun, being a word used in the place of or as a substitute for a noun, reflects the person, gender, and number of its antecedent whenever possible.

20.1 Les pronoms personnels

A. **Les pronoms sujets** (*subject pronouns*)

je	*I*
tu	*you*
il, elle	*he, she, it*
nous	*we*
vous	*you*
ils, elles	*they*

Tu and **vous** both mean *you*: **tu** is the familiar form, used to address children, relatives, close friends, and pets.

The subject pronoun **on** (see indefinite pronouns) indicates an unspecified quantity of persons and is always used with a verb in the third person singular.

B. **Les pronoms objets directs** (*direct object*)

The direct object pronoun stands for an object that receives the action of the verb without the means of a preposition:

il **me (m')** regarde
il **te (t')** regarde
il **le, la (l')** regarde
il **nous** regarde
il **vous** regarde
il **les** regarde

The direct object pronouns are used for things and persons. The pronoun **le** sometimes stands for an idea.

C. **Les pronoms objets indirects** (*indirect objects*)

The indirect object pronoun stands for an object that receives the action of the verb by means of the preposition **à** or **de**:

1. For persons only:

> il **me (m')** parle
> il **te (t')** parle
> il **lui** parle (masc. and fem.)
> il **nous** parle
> il **vous** parle
> il **leur** parle (masc. and fem.)

The indirect object pronoun replaces the entire prepositional phrase: Il **leur** parle. **(leur = à ses parents)**

2. For things only: **y**

Y replaces expressions starting with **à** or other prepositions:

Il va à **Rome**.	Il **y** va.
Elle est **au collège**.	Elle **y** est.
Il répond **aux questions**.	Il **y** répond.
Cette photo est-elle **dans le journal**?	Oui, elle **y** est.
Le vin est-il **sur la table**?	Oui, il **y** est.
La voiture est-elle **au garage**?	Non, elle n'**y** est pas.

The pronoun **y** replaces a noun preceded by a preposition indicating a position, except **de**.

3. **En** is the pronoun used to replace objects preceded by **de**:

Alice a-t-elle parlé **de son voyage**?	Oui, elle **en** a parlé.
Faites-vous **du tennis**?	Non, je n'**en** fais pas.
Êtes-vous content **de vos notes**?	Non, je n'**en** suis pas content.
Avez-vous envie **d'aller au cinéma**?	Non, je n'**en** ai pas envie.
Paul a-t-il besoin **de sa voiture**?	Oui, il **en** a besoin.
Mangez-vous **de la viande**?	Non, je n'**en** mange pas.
Prenez-vous **du sucre**?	Oui, j'**en** prends.

When the pronoun **en** replaces a noun preceded by an expression of quantity or a number, the expression or the number has to be repeated after the verb:

Avez-vous **des roses**?	Oui, j'**en** ai. Non, je n'**en** ai pas.
but:	
Avez-vous **une rose**?	Oui, j'**en** ai **une**.
Avez-vous **beaucoup de chance**?	Non, je n'**en** ai pas **beaucoup**.
Combien d'examens avez-vous?	Nous **en** avons **trois**.

En may replace a person used with a number, **des**, or an expression of quantity:

A-t-il **des amis**?	Non, il n'**en** a pas.
A-t-elle **beaucoup d'enfants**?	Oui, elle **en** a **beaucoup**.
Combien d'étudiants y a-t-il?	Il y **en** a **quarante**.

Both **y** and **en** are placed immediately in front of the infinitive if this is the verb they relate to. This rule applies to all object pronouns:

Allez-vous terminer **cet exercice**?	Je vais **le** terminer.
Désirez-vous faire **cette promenade**?	Je ne désire pas **la** faire.
Voudriez-vous aller **à Paris**?	Oui, je voudrais **y** aller.
As-tu vu **des accidents**?	Oui, j'**en** ai vu. Oui, je viens d'**en** voir.

With the name of a person, the preposition **de** is retained and the disjunctive pronoun is used: Il parle **d'eux**.

D. Object pronouns placement order in a sentence containing one or more pronouns.

Object pronouns are always placed before the verb except in the affirmative imperative.

SUJET	ne	me (m') te (t') se (s') nous vous se (s')	le (l') la (l') les	lui leur	y	en	VERBE ou AUXILIAIRE	pas rien plus jamais point guère	ADVERBE	PARTICIPE PASSÉ
		directs & indirects	directs	indirects						
		P	P-C	P	C	P-C				

P = personnes; C = choses

When the verb is in the affirmative imperative, the direct object pronoun precedes the indirect pronoun, the object pronouns being placed after the verb and joined to it by hyphens:

le	**lui**	**moi**	**y**	**en**
la	**leur**	**nous**		
les				

Moi is used in place of **me**, and **m'** before **en**. **Toi** is used in place of **te**, and **t'** before **en**:

> Pensez-**y**.   Rendez-**les-nous**.   Montrez-**la-moi**.
> Donnez-**m'en**.   Envoyez-**les-leur**.   Dites-**le lui**.

The reflexive pronoun **se** may act as direct and indirect pronoun for both genders, plural and singular, in the third person (see **les verbes pronominaux**).

E. **Les pronoms accentués ou disjonctifs** (*stressed, disjunctive*)

The disjunctive pronouns are so called because they are separated from the verb. They are used:

1. after prepositions:

> chez **moi**   chez **nous**
> chez **toi**   chez **vous**
> chez **lui**   chez **eux**
> chez **elle**   chez **elles**
> chez **soi**   chez **soi**

2. in comparisons:

> Charles est plus fort que **moi**.
> Il ne faut pas frapper un plus faible que **soi**.

3. in answers without a verb:

> Qui est là? – **Moi**.

4. after **c'est** and **ce sont**:

> C'est **lui** qui l'a dit.

after other tenses of **ce + être**:

> Ce fut **lui** qui parla.

5. for emphasis:

> **Moi**, je travaille; elle s'amuse.

6. in compound subjects:

> Nous y sommes allés, **lui et moi**.

7. when separated from the verb:

> **Eux** seuls sont coupables.

8. after **ne . . . que**:

> Je n'ai que **toi** dans la vie.

9. after **être à** to indicate ownership:

> Ce livre est à **lui**.

For emphasis the adjective **même** is often affixed to the pronoun:

> Il l'a fait **lui-même**.
> Ils y sont allés **eux-mêmes**.
> Cela se fait de **soi-même**.

20.2 Les pronoms possessifs (*possessive*)

A possessive pronoun replaces a noun modified by a possessive adjective:

mon livre	**le mien**	ma table	**la mienne**
ton livre	**le tien**	ta table	**la tienne**
son livre	**le sien**	sa table	**la sienne**
mes livres	**les miens**	mes tables	**les miennes**
tes livres	**les tiens**	tes tables	**les tiennes**
ses livres	**les siens**	ses tables	**les siennes**
notre livre	**le nôtre**	notre table	**la nôtre**
votre livre	**le vôtre**	votre table	**la vôtre**
leur livre	**le leur**	leur table	**la leur**
nos livres	**les nôtres**	nos tables	**les nôtres**
vos livres	**les vôtres**	vos tables	**les vôtres**
leurs livres	**les leurs**	leurs tables	**les leurs**

20.3 Les pronoms démonstratifs (*demonstrative*)

A. Variable demonstrative pronouns:

celui	**celle**	*this, that, the one*
ceux	**celles**	*these, those, the ones*

These pronouns refer to previously mentioned persons or things.
They never stand alone but are used:

1. before the preposition **de (du, des)**:

> la poésie de Verlaine   **celle de** Verlaine
> l'opinion des pays étrangers   **celle des** pays étrangers
> les discours de président   **ceux du** président

2. before a preposition followed by **qui** and a form of **lequel** (see relative pronouns):

> **Ceux pour qui** on travaille.
> Marie est **celle sur laquelle** on ne peut pas compter.
> **Ceux avec lesquels** on ne discute pas.

3. followed by the relative pronouns **qui, que,** or **dont**:

> **celui qui** chante   *the one who sings*
> **celle que** vous voyez   *the one (whom) you see*
> **ceux dont** vous m'avez parlé *the ones you spoke to me about*
> **celles que** vous désirez   *the ones you desire*

4. When these pronouns are linked to the particle **ci**, they refer to things that are close to the person speaking; and when linked to the particle **là**, they refer to things farther away:

> Je vois **celle-ci**, mais je ne vois pas **celle-là**.
> Je préfère **ceux-ci** à **celles-là**.

To avoid repetitions in a sentence, **celui-ci** and **celui-là** express the meanings of **the latter** and **the former**:

> Robert et Charles sont partis en voyage; **celui-ci** est allé
> plus loin que **celui-là**.

B. Invariable demonstrative pronouns **ceci, cela (ça), ce**

1. The pronouns **ceci** (*this*), **cela** (*that*) or the familiar form **ça** refer to general ideas already mentioned or to things not well defined:

> **Cela** me convient.   Je n'ai pas dit **ça**.
> **Cela (ça)** n'a aucune importance.   On n'a jamais vu
>   **cela (ça)**.
> **Ceci** ne m'intéresse pas, **cela** peut-être.

2. **Ce** or **c'** is the form generally used instead of **cela** and **ceci** before the verb **être**. It always precedes the third person (singular or plural) and its usual meaning is *it*.

Ce + être is used before:

A NOUN	**C'est un livre.**
	Ce sont mes livres.
	C'est un petit chien.
A PROPER NAME	**C'est Alice.**
A SUPERLATIVE	**Ce sont les meilleures.**
	C'est la plus jolie.
A DISJUNCTIVE PRONOUN	**Ce sont eux.**
	C'est moi.
A DEMONSTRATIVE PRONOUN	**C'est celui** de Paul.
A POSSESSIVE PRONOUN	**C'est le mien.**
	Ce sont les vôtres.

3. **c'est** and **il est**

The general rule is that **c'est** is followed by a noun whether or not accompanied by an adjective or an article:

> **C'est une classe** de français.
> **Ce sont mes parents.**
> **C'est une belle maison.**
> **Ce n'est** pas **Charles** qui a téléphoné.

Il est (or other third-person variations) is followed by an adjective:

> **Elle est charmante**, cette femme.
> **Ils sont intelligents.**
> **Il est fatigant** de travailler toute la journée.
> **Il est impossible** de traverser l'océan à pied.

Professions, religions, nationalities, and political affiliations are usually expressed in French by **il est**, noun used as an adjective, **c'est** is used when the noun is modified:

Il est américain.	C'est un Américain.
Ils sont catholiques.	Ce sont des catholiques.
Il est communiste.	C'est un communiste.
Il est dentiste.	C'est un dentiste.
Elle est juive.	C'est une juive.

C'est (third person singular only) may be followed by an adjective without a noun if **ce** refers to an idea already mentioned:

> Vous n'allez pas à Paris cet été? **C'est regrettable.**
> Vous travaillez sans être payé? **C'est incroyable!**

For **ce que, ce qui**, and **ce dont**, see relative pronouns.

20.4 Les pronoms relatifs

Relative pronouns are never omitted in French.

A. Simple relative pronouns   **qui, que, dont, quoi**

A relative pronoun introduces a clause which is in "relation" to a word in the principal clause; this word is called an antecedent.

1. **Qui** (*who, which, that*) is used for persons and things and functions as subject of the verb in the subordinate clause. **Qui** can never become **qu'**:

> La personne **qui** a téléphoné n'a pas donné son nom.
> La voiture **qui** est devant la porte ne m'appartient pas.
> Ce sont les étudiants **qui** ont protesté.

Qui (*whom*) is also used as the object after most prepositions but only when it refers to persons:

> Le médecin **à qui** j'ai téléphoné était trop occupé.
> La personne **chez qui** vous avez dîné est mon amie.
> Les gens **avec qui** ils ont voyagé sont très riches.

After **sans, entre,** and **parmi,** a form of lequel (compound relative pronoun) replaces **qui**:

> Les candidats **parmi lesquels** il faut choisir sont ici.

After the preposition **de**, the pronoun **dont** is generally used (see below).

2. **Que** is used for persons or things and functions as a direct object. It can mean *whom, which,* or *that*:

> L'avion **que** je prendrai est un jet.
> Le musicien **que** nous écoutons est célèbre.
> Les chaussures **que** nous voulons acheter sont chères.

Que becomes **qu'** before a word beginning with a vowel or mute **h**:

> J'aime les histoires **qu'elle** raconte.
> Les devoirs **qu'ils** remettent sont pleins de fautes.

3. **Quoi** is used when the antecedent has no gender or number and after a preposition:

> Voilà **à quoi** vous pensez!
> Il n'y a pas **de quoi** se vanter.

4. **Dont** (*whose, of whom, of which*) refers to persons and things and contains the preposition **de**. Therefore, it is the equivalent of **de qui**, **de quoi** and the compound relative pronouns **duquel**, **de laquelle**, **desquels**, and **desquelles**:

L'argent **dont** on a besoin . . .	(avoir besoin de)
Le résultat **dont** je suis fier . . .	(être fier de)
L'écrivain **dont** les oeuvres sont célèbres . . .	(possession)
Le voyage **dont** il a envie . . .	(avoir envie de)
La femme **dont** je parle . . .	(parler de)
L'accident **dont** il est question . . .	(il est question de)
L'expérience **dont** il s'agit . . .	(il s'agit de)
L'entrevue **dont** nous avions peur . . .	(avoir peur de)
Le crayon **dont** la pointe est cassée . . .	(possession)
L'acteur **dont** vous avez entendu parler . . .	(entendre parler de)

Dont may *not* be used when the relative pronoun follows a noun introduced by a preposition and has a relation of possession with the antecedent of the relative pronoun. Instead, **de qui, duquel**, etc. are used:

Le rocher **à l'ombre duquel** nous dormons (l'ombre du rocher)
La maison **à la porte de laquelle** j'ai frappé (la porte de la maison)
Le président **contre le discours duquel** j'ai protesté (le discours du président)

5. **ce qui** (*what, that which*), **ce que** (*what, that which*), and **ce dont** (*of which, about what*)

If the relative pronouns **qui** (subject), **que** (object), and **dont** (object requiring the preposition **de**) have no noun or pronoun antecedent, **ce** functions as antecedent before the relative pronoun:

> Dites-moi **ce qui** vous intéresse.
> Je sais **ce qui** vous ennuie.
> **Ce que** je voudrais, c'est une nouvelle voiture.
> Je n'ai pas fait **ce qu'**elle m'a demandé.
> Il a bien travaillé, **ce dont** il est content.

Ce qui and **ce que** replace the interrogative forms of **qu'est-ce qui?** and **qu'est-ce que?** in subordinate clauses and in reported speech (see **discours indirect**):

> **Qu'est-ce qui** vous intéresse?   **Ce qui** m'intéresse c'est . . .
>   Je sais **ce qui** m'intéresse.

B. **Les pronoms relatifs composés** (*compound relative pronouns*)

The compound relative pronouns must agree in gender and number with their antecedent.

	SINGULAR		PLURAL	
	MASC.	FEM.	MASC.	FEM.
Contracted with de Contracted with à	lequel duquel auquel	laquelle	lesquels desquels auxquels	lesquelles desquelles auxquelles

The compound relative pronouns must always be used for things after a preposition. **Quoi** is rarely used. **Qui** is used for persons (see above), although it is possible to use the compound relative pronouns for persons to avoid ambiguity:

> Voici le journal **dans lequel** se trouve cet article.
> Los Angeles est une ville **autour de laquelle** il y a des montagnes.
> Les valises **dans lesquelles** se trouvaient mes meilleurs vêtements sont perdues.
> Les cours **auxquels** j'assiste sont intéressants.
> Le fils d'Alice, **lequel** était malade, vient d'arriver. (To avoid ambiguity, **lequel** is used instead of **qui**.)
> La Loire est un fleuve **au bord duquel** il y a de beaux châteaux.
> Les fautes **auxquelles** il n'a pas fait attention sont graves.

Où often replaces **à**, **dans**, **sur**, **au bord de**, **autour de**, etc. + a compound relative pronoun in expressions of time and place (for things only):

> Les valises **où** se trouvaient . . .
> La Loire est un fleuve **où** il y a de beaux châteaux.
> Le siècle **où** (dans lequel) nous vivons est inquiétant.

20.5 Les pronoms indéfinis

Some indefinite pronouns are used as adjectives (see indefinite adjectives). The purely pronominal are:

A. **on**   This pronoun indicates that the action is done by one or several unspecified persons. According to the context, it has the value of *one, we, you, they, someone, people,* etc. It is always the subject and used with a verb in the third person singular:

> **On boit** beaucoup de vin en France.
> **Fume-t-on** dans les cinémas?

On ne me l'a pas dit.
Et puis **on** ne **sait** jamais.
On vient de faire passer un bon film.
On est triste quand **on perd** un ami.

L'on is used after **si, ou, où, et**, and **que**, but never when the following word starts with an **l**:

Si **l'on** veut avoir des amis, il ne faut pas être égoïste.
Quoi que **l'on** dise.
but:
On comprendra **si on lit** cet article.

B. **Chacun** and **chacune** (*each one*) are always singular and correspond to the indefinite adjective **chaque**:

Il y a beaucoup de classes et dans **chacune** il y a beaucoup d'étudiants.
Chacun fait ce qu'il veut dans cette famille.

C. **Quelqu'un, quelqu'une** (*someone*), **quelques-uns** and **quelques-unes** (*some of them*) correspond to the indefinite adjective **quelque(s)**:

J'aime ces photographies; **quelques-unes** sont splendides.
Quelqu'un est venu vous voir.

The negative of **quelqu'un** is **personne** (see **négation**).

D. **Quelque chose** (*something*)   The negative form is **rien** (see **négation**):

Avez-vous **quelque chose** de bon à manger?

	also:	**autre chose**	*something else*
		grand-chose	*much*
		peu de chose	*not much, very little*

E. **Quiconque** (*anybody*) is always masculine singular:

Il m'aidera mieux que **quiconque**.
Pas un mot à **quiconque**!

F. **Tout, toute** (*all, the whole*), **tous, toutes** (*all of them*) correspond to the indefinite adjectives having the same forms.

Tout est fini.	*everything*
Elle comprend **tout**.	*everything*

(la lettre) Je l'ai lue **toute**.	*I read it all.*
Elles sont **toutes** venues.	*all of them*
Tes amis sont **tous** là.	*all of them*

In **tous** (pronoun), the s is pronounced. Note the following expressions:

tout le monde	*everybody*
tout à fait	*completely*
tout à l'heure	*in a while, a while ago*
tout de suite	*right away*
tout à coup	*suddenly*
une fois pour toutes	*once and for all*
tous ensemble	*all together*
pas du tout	*not at all*

G. autre, autrui

Autre corresponds to the indefinite adjective and is always preceded by an article:

C'est **un autre** qui a payé.	*another one*
Une autre à sa place serait restée.	*another one*
L'un a ri, **l'autre** a pleuré.	*the other*
Les uns s'amusent, **les autres** étudient.	*(the) others*
(*Some have fun, some study*.)	

Autrui (*others, other people*) usually follows a preposition:

Respectez le bien **d'autrui**.
Ne fais pas **à autrui** ce que tu ne voudrais pas qu'on te fît.

H. **Même** as a pronoun is preceded by the definite article:

Ce n'est pas le livre que je vous ai prêté. Oui, c'est **le même**.
Ce sont les mêmes personnes? Oui, ce sont **les mêmes**.

I. For **personne**, **rien**, and **aucun**, see **négation** and **adjectifs indéfinis**.

20.6 Les pronoms interrogatifs

A. The simple interrogative pronouns

1. For persons: **qui?** *who? whom? whose?*

Subject:	**Qui** est à la porte?
	Qui veut du café?

Direct object: **Qui** regardez-vous?
           Qui invitez-vous ce soir?

After a preposition: **Avec qui** sort-elle?
           A qui écrivent-ils?
           Chez qui allons-nous ce soir?

2. For things: **qu'est-ce qui?**, **qu'est-ce que?**, **que?**, **quoi?** *what?*

Subject: **Qu'est-ce qui** est sur la table?
           Qu'est-ce qui est arrivé?

Direct object: **Qu'est-ce que** vous regardez?
           Que regardez-vous? (inversion)
           Qu'est-ce qu'il a fait?
           Qu'a-t-il fait? (inversion)
           Qu'est-ce que vous demandez?
           Que demandez-vous? (inversion)

After a preposition: **A quoi** pensez-vous?
           De quoi parle-t-elle?
           Sur quoi mettez-vous ces disques?

B. The compound interrogative pronouns

They are identical in form with the compound relative pronouns:

lequel?	**laquelle?**	**lesquels?**	**lesquelles?**
duquel?	**de laquelle?**	**desquels?**	**desquelles?**
auquel?	**à laquelle?**	**auxquels?**	**auxquelles?**

Lequel avez-vous vu?	*Which ones did you see?*
Laquelle est votre femme?	*Which one is your wife?*
Desquels parlez-vous?	*Of which ones are you speaking?*
Auquel avez-vous posé la question?	*Of which one did you ask the question?*

The forms **qui est-ce qui?** as subject and **qui est-ce que?** as object often replace **qui?** for persons:

Qui est à la porte?	**Qui est-ce qui** est à la porte?
Qui invitez-vous?	**Qui est-ce que** vous invitez? (no inversion)

21 Il y a, voici, voilà

A. **il y a** The negative form is **il n'y a pas** and the interrogative form is **y a-t-il?**
Il y a is a common idiomatic expression indicating existence and means *there is* or
there are. (For the use of **il y a** in expressions indicating time, see the verb section):

> **Il y a** un livre sur la table.
> **Y a-t-il** une personne à la porte?
> **Il n'y a pas** de [1] compositions à remettre.

B. **Voici** (*here is, here are*) comes from **vois + ici**, meaning "see here," and **voilà**
(*there is, there are*) comes from **vois + là** meaning "see there." They are used to
point out objects, persons, and concepts:

> **Voilà** une porte.
> **Voici** Charles.
> **Voilà** une ambition peu commune.

For the use of **voici** and **voilà** in expressions indicating time, see the verb section.

---

[1] **des** becomes **de** in a negative sentence with **il y a.**

22 La ponctuation

.	le point
,	la virgule
:	les deux points
;	le point-virgule
« »	les guillemets
?	le point d'interrogation
!	le point d'exclamation
...	les points de suspension
( )	les parenthèses
—	le tiret ou le trait d'union

23 Majuscules et minuscules (capitalization)

Capital letters are less frequently used in French than in English.

Capitalize only:

> the first word in a sentence
> proper names
> the names of nationals of a country and the residents of a city:
> **une Anglaise**;　**les Français**;　**les Parisiens**.

Do not capitalize:

the days of the week	Aujourd'hui c'est **lundi**.
the months	Nous sommes en **janvier**.
languages	Le **français** est difficile.
religions	les **catholiques**
members of political parties	Ce sont des **socialistes**.
adjectives formed from nouns	une compagnie **américaine**
je (unless it is the first word)	Hier, **je** lui ai parlé.

24   Le verbe <u>être</u>

Indicatif

	PRÉSENT	IMPARFAIT	PASSÉ SIMPLE	FUTUR
je	suis	étais	fus	serai
tu	es	étais	fus	seras
il	est	était	fut	sera
nous	sommes	étions	fûmes	serons
vous	êtes	étiez	fûtes	serez
ils	sont	étaient	furent	seront

	PASSÉ COMPOSÉ	PLUS-QUE-PARFAIT	FUTUR ANTÉRIEUR
j'	ai été	avais été	aurai été
tu	as été	avais été	auras été
il	a été	avait été	aura été
nous	avons été	avions été	aurons été
vous	avez été	aviez été	aurez été
ils	ont été	avaient été	auront été

Conditionnel

	PRÉSENT	PASSÉ
je	serais	aurais été
tu	serais	aurais été
il	serait	aurait été
nous	serions	aurions été
vous	seriez	auriez été
ils	seraient	auraient été

Impératif

sois
soyons
soyez

Subjonctif

	PRÉSENT	PASSÉ	IMPARFAIT
que je	sois	aie été	fusse
que tu	sois	aies été	fusses
qu'il	soit	ait été	fût
que nous	soyons	ayons été	fussions
que vous	soyez	ayez été	fussiez
qu'ils	soient	aient été	fussent

Infinitif: être

Infinitif passé: avoir été

Participe présent: étant

Participe passé: été

25 Le verbe <u>avoir</u>

Indicatif

	PRÉSENT	IMPARFAIT	PASSÉ SIMPLE	FUTUR
j'	ai	avais	eus	aurai
tu	as	avais	eus	auras
il	a	avait	eut	aura
nous	avons	avions	eûmes	aurons
vous	avez	aviez	eûtes	aurez
ils	ont	avaient	eurent	auront

	PASSÉ COMPOSÉ	PLUS-QUE-PARFAIT	FUTUR ANTÉRIEUR
j'	ai eu	avais eu	aurai eu
tu	as eu	avais eu	auras eu
il	a eu	avait eu	aura eu
nous	avons eu	avions eu	aurons eu
vous	avez eu	aviez eu	aurez eu
ils	ont eu	avaient eu	auront eu

Conditionnel

	PRÉSENT	PASSÉ
j'	aurais	aurais eu
tu	aurais	aurais eu
il	aurait	aurait eu
nous	aurions	aurions eu
vous	auriez	auriez eu
ils	auraient	auraient eu

Impératif

aie
ayons
ayez

Subjonctif

	PRÉSENT	PASSÉ	IMPARFAIT
que j'	aie	aie eu	eusse
que tu	aies	aies eu	eusses
qu'il	ait	ait eu	eût
que nous	ayons	ayons eu	eussions
que vous	ayez	ayez eu	eussiez
qu'ils	aient	aient eu	eussent

Infinitif: avoir

Infinitif passé: avoir eu

Participe présent: ayant

Participe passé: eu

26 Idiomatic expressions with avoir

avoir faim	to be hungry
avoir soif	to be thirsty
avoir chaud	to be warm, hot
avoir froid	to be cold
avoir sommeil	to be sleepy
avoir tort	to be wrong
avoir raison	to be right
avoir lieu	to take place
avoir bonne mine	to look well
avoir envie de	to want, to have a fancy for
avoir besoin de	to be in need, to need
avoir peur de	to be afraid of
avoir honte de	to be ashamed of
avoir coutume de	to be in the habit of
avoir 20 ans	to be 20 years old
avoir l'air	to seem
avoir mal à la tête	to have a headache
avoir mal aux dents	to have a toothache
avoir mal à la gorge	to have a sore throat
avoir de la chance	to be lucky
avoir de l'esprit	to be witty
avoir la parole	to have the floor
avoir l'occasion	to have the opportunity
avoir l'intention de + infinitif	to intend
avoir du mal à + infinitif	to have difficulty
avoir le mal de mer	to be seasick
avoir le mal du pays	to be homesick
avoir à + infinitif	to have to
avoir beau + infinitif	however much, in vain

27 Idiomatic expressions with être

j'y suis!	*I get it!*
j'en suis!	*I am game!*
soit	*so be it, agreed*
soit dit . . .	*be it said . . .*
où en sommes-nous?	*How far have we got?*
cela m'est égal	*It is all the same to me.*
c'est égal	*It doesn't matter.*
être enrhumé	*to have a cold*
être d'accord	*to agree*
être au courant	*to be informed*
être agée de 20 ans	*to be 20 years old*
être de bonne humeur	*to be in a good humor*
ne pas être dans son assiette	*to be out of sorts*
Je suis de votre avis.	*I agree with you.*
être amoureux de	*to be in love with*
être fou de	*to be crazy about*
être un bon vivant	*to be fond of good living*
être en train de	*to be in the act of, to be engaged in*
être à son aise	*to be comfortable, well-off*
être passioné pour	*to be very fond of*
ce n'est pas la peine de . . .	*don't bother to . . .*
quelle heure est-il?	*What time is it?*

28 Verbes en -er: premier groupe

Conjugaison du verbe type: **parler**

INDICATIF

	PRÉSENT	IMPARFAIT	PASSÉ SIMPLE	FUTUR
je	parle	parlais	parlai	parlerai
tu	parles	parlais	parlas	parleras
il	parle	parlait	parla	parlera
nous	parlons	parlions	parlâmes	parlerons
vous	parlez	parliez	parlâtes	parlerez
ils	parlent	parlaient	parlèrent	parleront

	PASSÉ COMPOSÉ	PLUS-QUE-PARFAIT	FUTUR ANTÉRIEUR
j'	ai parlé	avais parlé	aurai parlé
tu	as parlé	avais parlé	auras parlé
il	a parlé	avait parlé	aura parlé
nous	avons parlé	avions parlé	aurons parlé
vous	avez parlé	aviez parlé	aurez parlé
ils	ont parlé	avaient parlé	auront parlé

CONDITIONNEL

	PRÉSENT	PASSÉ
je	parlerais	aurais parlé
tu	parlerais	aurais parlé
il	parlerait	aurait parlé
nous	parlerions	aurions parlé
vous	parleriez	auriez parlé
ils	parleraient	auraient parlé

IMPÉRATIF

parle
parlons
parlez

SUBJONCTIF

	PRÉSENT	PASSÉ	IMPARFAIT
que je	parle	aie parlé	parlasse
que tu	parles	aies parlé	parlasses
qu'il	parle	ait parlé	parlât
que nous	parlions	ayons parlé	parlassions
que vous	parliez	ayez parlé	parlassiez
qu'ils	parlent	aient parlé	parlassent

INFINITIF:	parler
INFINITIF PASSÉ:	avoir parlé
PARTICIPE PRÉSENT:	parlant
PARTICIPE PASSÉ:	parlé

Particularités orthographiques
(orthographical changes)
29 premier groupe

The stems of some of the verbs of the first group undergo certain orthographical changes.

A. Verbs ending in **-cer** change **c** to **ç** before the vowels **a, o, u**:

commencer:	nous commençons	en commençant
effacer:	nous effaçons	en effaçant
placer:	nous plaçons	en plaçant

B. Verbs ending in **-ger** add an **e** after **g** before **a, o, u**:

manger:	nous mangeons	en mangeant
changer:	nous changeons	en changeant
voyager:	nous voyageons	en voyageant

C. Verbs ending in **-eter** and **-eler** double the **l** or **t** before mute **e**:

jeter:	je jette	ils jettent
appeler:	j'appelle	ils appellent

Exceptions: **acheter, crocheter, haleter, geler, dégeler, congeler, surgeler, modeler, ciseler, peler, marteler**

These verbs change the **e** of the stem to **è** when the ending of the verb begins with mute **e**:

acheter:	j'achète	il achètera
geler:	je gèle	il gèlerait

D. Verbs ending in **-ecer, -emer, -ener, -eper, -eser, -ever, -evrer** change **e** to **è** before the ending of the verb beginning with mute **e**:

amener:	j'amène	ils amèneront
se promener:	elle se promène	tu te promèneras
enlever:	j'enlève	ils enlèvent

E. Verbs with an **é** in the last syllable of the stem change this **é** to **è** when the ending begins with mute **e**. This occurs only in two tenses, **indicatif présent** and **subjonctif présent**:

espérer:	j'espère	qu'il espère
répéter:	je répète	qu'il répète
posséder:	je possède	qu'elles possèdent

F. Verbs ending in **-ayer, -oyer, -uyer** change y to **i** before mute e:

employer:	j'emploie	ils emploieront
ennuyer:	ils ennuient	nous ennuierions
payer:	ils paient	il paiera

The verbs in **-ayer**, however, may keep the **y**:

payer:	ils payent	il payera

Verbes en -ir: deuxième groupe (participe présent en -issant)

30

Conjugaison du verbe type: **finir**

INDICATIF

	PRÉSENT	IMPARFAIT	PASSÉ SIMPLE	FUTUR
je	finis	finissais	finis	finirai
tu	finis	finissais	finis	finiras
il	finit	finissait	finit	finira
nous	finissons	finissions	finîmes	finirons
vous	finissez	finissiez	finîtes	finirez
ils	finissent	finissaient	finirent	finiront

	PASSÉ COMPOSÉ	PLUS-QUE-PARFAIT	FUTUR ANTÉRIEUR
j'	ai fini	avais fini	aurai fini
tu	as fini	avais fini	auras fini
il	a fini	avait fini	aura fini
nous	avons fini	avions fini	aurons fini
vous	avez fini	aviez fini	aurez fini
ils	ont fini	avaient fini	auront fini

CONDITIONNEL

	PRÉSENT	PASSÉ
je	finirais	aurais fini
tu	finirais	aurais fini
il	finirait	aurait fini
nous	finirions	aurions fini
vous	finiriez	auriez fini
ils	finiraient	auraient fini

IMPÉRATIF

finis
finissons
finissez

[86]

SUBJONCTIF

	PRÉSENT	PASSÉ	IMPARFAIT
que je	finisse	aie fini	finisse
que tu	finisses	aies fini	finisses
qu'il	finisse	ait fini	finît
que nous	finissions	ayons fini	finissions
que vous	finissiez	ayez fini	finissez
qu'ils	finissent	aient fini	finissent

INFINITIF: **finir**

INFINITIF PASSÉ: **avoir fini**

PARTICIPE PRÉSENT: **finissant**

PARTICIPE PASSÉ: **fini**

31
List of the most common verbs in the second group (-ir)

abasourdir
abêtir
abolir
aboutir
abrutir
accomplir
adoucir
affaiblir
affermir
affranchir
agir
agrandir
aguerrir
ahurir
aigrir
alourdir
amincir
amoindrir
amortir
anéantir
aplanir
aplatir
appauvrir
applaudir
approfondir
arrondir
assagir
assainir
assombrir
assortir
assoupir
assouplir
assourdir
assujettir

attendrir
atterrir
attiédir
avachir
avilir
bannir
bâtir
bénir
blanchir
blêmir
bleuir
blondir
blottir
bondir
brandir
brunir
choisir
chérir
compartir
crépir
croupir
dégarnir
dégarpir
dégourdir
démunir
dépolir
désassortir
désobéir
désunir
divertir
durcir
éblouir
éclaircir
élargir

embellir
emplir
endolorir
enfouir
engloutir
engourdir
enhardir
enlaidir
ennoblir
enorgueillir
enrichir
ensevelir
envahir
épaissir
établir
étourdir
(s')évanouir
faiblir
farcir
finir
fléchir
flétrir
fournir
franchir
frémir
garantir
garnir
grandir
grossir
guérir
intervertir
invertir
investir
jaillir

jaunir	polir	rétrécir
languir	pourrir	réunir
maigrir	punir	réussir
maudire (participe passé: **maudit**)	raccourcir	rôtir
meutrir	raidir	rougir
moisir	radoucir	rugir
munir	raffermir	saisir
mûrir	rafraîchir	salir
noircir	ragaillardir	subir
nourrir	rajeunir	surgir
obéir	ralentir	ternir
obscurcir	rebâtir	trahir
pâlir	réfléchir	travestir
pâtir	refroidir	unir
périr	remplir	vernir
pervertir	rétablir	vieillir
pétrir	retentir	vomir

32 Verbes en -andre, -endre, -ondre, -erdre, -ordre[1]

Conjugaison du verbe type: **vendre**

INDICATIF

	PRÉSENT	IMPARFAIT	PASSÉ SIMPLE	FUTUR
je	vends	vendais	vendis	vendrai
tu	vends	vendais	vendis	vendras
il	vend	vendait	vendit	vendra
nous	vendons	vendions	vendîmes	vendrons
vous	vendez	vendiez	vendîtes	vendrez
ils	vendent	vendaient	vendirent	vendront

	PASSÉ COMPOSÉ	PLUS-QUE-PARFAIT	FUTUR ANTÉRIEUR
j'	ai vendu	avais vendu	aurai vendu
tu	as vendu	avais vendu	auras vendu
il	a vendu	avait vendu	aura vendu
nous	avons vendu	avions vendu	aurons vendu
vous	avez vendu	aviez vendu	aurez vendu
ils	ont vendu	avaient vendu	auront vendu

CONDITIONNEL

	PRESÉNT	PASSÉ
je	vendrais	aurais vendu
tu	vendrais	aurais vendu
il	vendrait	aurait vendu
nous	vendrions	aurions vendu
vous	vendriez	auriez vendu
ils	vendraient	auraient vendu

[1] Exception: **prendre** (and compounds)

IMPÉRATIF

vends
vendons
vendez

SUBJONCTIF

	PRÉSENT	PASSÉ	IMPARFAIT
que je	vende	aie vendu	vendisse
que tu	vendes	aies vendu	vendisses
qu'il	vende	ait vendu	vendît
que nous	vendions	ayons vendu	vendissions
que vous	vendiez	ayez vendu	vendissiez
qu'ils	vendent	aient vendu	vendissent

INFINITIF:	vendre
INFINITIF PASSÉ:	avoir vendu
PARTICIPE PRÉSENT:	vendant
PARTICIPE PASSÉ:	vendu

33 Le présent de l'indicatif

33.1 Formation

A. For the two regular conjugations, the present indicative is formed by dropping the infinitive ending (**terminaison**) and adding the present indicative ending for each conjugation:

	parler		**finir**
je	parle	je	finis
tu	parles	tu	finis
il	parle	il	finit
nous	parlons	nous	finissons
vous	parlez	vous	finissez
ils	parlent	ils	finissent

B. Most irregular verbs (third group) have the following endings in common:

	voir
je	vois
tu	vois
il	voit
nous	voyons
vous	voyez
ils	voient

C. With verbs ending in **-dre**, the third person singular ends in **-d** rather than **-t**.

D. Exceptions are **avoir, être, aller, faire, dire**.

E. The endings of the first and second persons singular of **pouvoir, vouloir, valoir** are **-x** instead of **-s**:

je peux	je veux	je vaux
tu peux	tu veux	tu vaux

For stem (radical) changes, see the table of conjugations of irregular verbs.

[92]

33.2 Emploi

A. An action going on at the present:

Je **mange** en ce moment.   *I'm eating now.*
Je vous **écoute**.   *I'm listening to you.*

B. Habitual or constant actions or situations:

Je **vais** à l'église le dimanche.

C. In **depuis, il y a . . . que** and **voilà . . . que** constructions (see these words in the index).

D. For future action if indicated by context:

Je **sors** ce soir   *I'm going out tonight.*

34 L'imparfait de l'indicatif

34.1 Formation

All verbs have the same endings in this tense:

je	parl**ais**
tu	parl**ais**
il	parl**ait**
nous	parl**ions**
vous	parl**iez**
ils	parl**aient**

All verbs (except **être**) derive the imperfect stem from the first person plural of the present indicative by dropping the **-ons** ending:

nous parl~~ons~~	je parl**ais**, etc.
nous finiss~~ons~~	je finiss**ais**, etc.
nous vend~~ons~~	je vend**ais**, etc.
nous all~~ons~~	j'all**ais**, etc.
nous buv~~ons~~	je buv**ais**, etc.
nous connaiss~~ons~~	je connaiss**ais**, etc.

34.2 Emploi

There are several tenses in French to express past time. Each of these tenses has, besides the general role of expressing the past, specific functions. The **imparfait** is used:

A. To describe repeated or habitual actions in the past. In English this is usually expressed by *used to* or a progressive construction. These actions are visualized as continuing:

> Il **allait** au cinéma tous les soirs.
> Il **fumait** beaucoup quand il **était** jeune.
> Nous **prenions** nos repas au restaurant.

[94]

B. To describe an action that was going on at the time when another action took place:

> Mon père **regardait** la télévision quand je suis entré.

C. To describe physical or mental conditions:

> Ce professeur qui **avait** des cheveux blancs **était** très sympathique.

D. To describe weather conditions or nature:

> Le soleil **brillait** et il **pleuvait** en même temps.

E. In **depuis, il y a . . . que** and **voilà . . . que** constructions (see the index).

F. To replace the present (see **le discours indirect**).

34.3 Le passé récent: **venir de** + infinitif

A. The recent past is expressed with the present tense of the verb **venir de** followed by an infinitive: Il **vient de finir** son travail.

B. An action that took place immediately before another past action is expressed by the imperfect: Il **venait de sortir** quand vous avez téléphoné.

35 Le passé composé

35.1 Formation

To form compound tenses in French, combine the simple tenses of **avoir** or être with the past participle of the verb to be conjugated in compound tenses.

The **passé composé**, being a compound tense, is formed with the present tense of **avoir** or être (auxiliary verbs) and the past participle of the verb to be conjugated. Most verbs are conjugated with **avoir**.

A. Verbs conjugated with **être**:

1.

arriver	**partir**
aller	**venir** (and compounds)
entrer	**sortir**
rentrer	**retourner**
descendre	**monter**
mourir	**naître**
tomber	**rester**

2. All the reflexive verbs (see **les verbes pronominaux**).

3. In the passive voice (see **la forme passive**).

B. **Participe passé**

1. The past participle of regular verbs is formed by changing the infinitive ending **-er** to **-é** and **-ir** to **-i**:

parl¢¢	parlé	fin¢¢	fini
mang¢¢	mangé	chois¢¢	choisi
étudi¢¢	étudié	grand¢¢	grandi

2. Past participle of irregular verbs (third group):

in **-u**

battre	**battu**
boire	**bu**

conclure	**conclu**
connaître	**connu**
coudre	**cousu**
croire	**cru**
devoir	**dû**
émouvoir	**ému**
falloir	**fallu**
lire	**lu**
plaire	**plu**
pleuvoir	**plu**
recevoir	**reçu**
pouvoir	**pu**
résoudre	**résolu**
rompre	**rompu**
savoir	**su**
taire	**tu**
tenir (and compounds)	**tenu**
vaincre	**vaincu**
valoir	**valu**
vendre	**vendu**
venir (and compounds)	**venu**
vêtir	**vêtu**
vivre	**vécu**
voir (and compounds)	**vu**
vouloir	**voulu**

in -i

cueillir	**cueilli**
haïr	**haï**
luire	**lui**
nuire	**nui**
rire	**ri**
fuir	**fui**
dormir	**dormi**
sourire	**souri**
suffire	**suffi**
suivre	**suivi**

in -it

conduire	**conduit**
décrire	**décrit**

dire	**dit**
écrire	**écrit**
produire	**produit**
traduire	**traduit**

in **-is**

aquérir	**acquis**
asseoir	**assis**
conquérir	**conquis**
comprendre	**compris**
mettre	**mis**
prendre	**pris**

in **-ert**

couvrir	**couvert**
découvrir	**découvert**
offrir	**offert**
ouvrir	**ouvert**
recouvrir	**recouvert**
souffrir	**souffert**

in **-int**

atteindre	**atteint**
craindre	**craint**
joindre	**joint**
peindre	**peint**

entirely irregular

avoir	**eu**
distraire	**distrait**
extraire	**extrait**
faire	**fait**
naître	**né**
mourir	**mort**

35.2 Emploi

The **passé composé** is used to relate a completed past event or a sudden and momentary occurrence. The time limit is expressed or implied by the context. Its emphasis is narrative whereas the **imparfait** is mainly descriptive:

Hier matin, nous **avons pris** l'autobus.
Elle **a fini** tous ses exercices.
Nous **avons** beaucoup **étudié** pour les examens.
Mon père ne m'**a** pas **donné** sa voiture.
Il **a fallu** travailler pendant les vacances.
Marie **est partie** sans me dire au revoir.
Avez-vous **reçu** beaucoup de cadeaux?
Dimanche dernier, nous **sommes allés** faire du ski.
Je les **ai vus** très souvent.
Ils **ont bu** trop de vin et cela leur **a coûté** cher.

The **passé composé** is used primarily in conversation and informal writing. The **passé simple** is its equivalent literary tense (see that tense).

35.3 Accord du participe passé

A. In all compound tenses with the auxiliary verb **avoir**, the past participle must agree in gender and in number with the direct object if it *precedes* the verb. The past participle remains invariable if there is no direct object or if the direct object follows the verb:

Voici les livres **que** vous avez achetés.
(agreement: **que** is the direct object and its antecedent is **les livres**).

Reprenez vos compositions, je **les** ai corrigées.
(agreement: **les** is the direct object and its antecedent is **les compositions**).

Il a lu la leçon avant de sortir.
(no agreement: **la leçon** is the direct object and it follows the verb).

Nous avons parlé toute la soirée.
(no agreement: no direct object).

Elles leur ont téléphoné hier soir.
(no agreement: **leur** is an indirect object).

B. If **être** is the auxiliary verb, the past participle must agree with the subject (see also **verbes pronominaux**):

Elles sont allées à New York.
Alice est née en 1950.
Sont-**ils** arrivés en bateau?
Malgré le froid, **nous** ne sommes pas tombés malades.

Monter, descendre, sortir, rentrer may sometimes have a direct object. In that case the auxiliary verb is **avoir**:

J'ai monté les bagages.
(The meaning of **monter** is not *to climb*, but *to take upstairs*).

Il **les** a rentrés.
(*He brought them back in.* The meaning is not *to come back*).

Il n'a pas sorti son chien dans la pluie.
(The meaning is not *to go out,* but *to take out*).

36 Le passé simple

The **passé simple** is formed by dropping the ending of the infinitive and adding the following endings:

je	parlai	je	finis	je	voulus
tu	parlas	tu	finis	tu	voulus
il	parla	il	finit	il	voulut
nous	parlâmes	nous	finîmes	nous	voulûmes
vous	parlâtes	vous	finîtes	vous	voulûtes
ils	parlèrent	ils	finirent	ils	voulurent

The **passé simple** expresses an action entirely completed in the past. It is a narrative tense used in literary contexts and very seldom in conversation. The **passé simple** is replaced by the **passé composé** in conversation.

37 Le plus-que-parfait

37.1 Formation

The **plus-que-parfait** is a compound tense. It is formed with the imperfect tense of **avoir** or **être** and the past participle of the verb to be conjugated:

> Il avait parlé.
> (no agreement: no direct object).
>
> **Nous** étions sortis.
> (agreement with subject)

37.2 Emploi

The pluperfect indicates that an action took place before another action in the past or that a condition existed before another past event:

Quand je suis entré, mon frère mangeait le repas que ma mère lui **avait préparé**.
When I came in, my brother was eating the meal that my mother had prepared for him.
Il **avait fait** beau toute la journée quand tout à coup il a commencé a pleuvoir.

The following two passages from *L'Étranger* by Albert Camus illustrate the use of the **passé composé**, the **imparfait**, and the **plus-que-parfait**.

Emphasis on the **passé composé**:

J'ai **dîné** chez Céleste. J'avais déjà commencé à manger lorsqu'il **est entré** une bizarre petite femme qui m'**a demandé** si elle pouvait s'asseoir à ma table. Naturellement elle le pouvait. Elle avait des gestes saccadés et des yeux brillants dans une petite figure de pomme. Elle s'**est débarrassée** de sa jaquette, s'**est assise** et **a consulté** fiévreusement la carte. Elle **a appelé** Céleste et **a commandé** immédiatement tous ses plats d'une voix à la fois précise et précipitée. En attendant les hors-d'œuvre, elle **a ouvert** son sac, en **a sorti** un petit carré de papier et un crayon, **a fait** d'avance l'addition, pui **a tiré** d'un gousset, augmentée du pourboire, la somme exacte qu'elle **a placée** devant elle. A ce moment on lui **a apporté** des hors-d'œuvre qu'elle **a engloutis** à toute vitesse. En attendant le plat suivant, elle **a** encore **sorti** de son sac un crayon bleu et un magazine qui donnait les programmes radiophoniques de la semaine.

Emphasis on the **imparfait** and the **plus-que-parfait**:

J'**étais** accroupi sur mon lit et Salamano s'**était assis** sur une chaise devant la table. Il me **faisait** face et il **avait** ses deux mains sur les genoux. Il **avait gardé** son vieux feutre. Il **mâchonnait** des bouts de phrases sous sa moustache jaunie. Il m'**ennuyait** un peu, mais je n'**avais** rien à faire et je n'**avais** pas sommeil. Pour dire quelque chose, je l'ai interrogé sur son chien. Il m'a dit qu'il l'**avait eu** après la mort de sa femme. Il s'**était marié** assez tard. Dans sa jeunesse, il **avait eu** envie de faire du théâtre: au régiment il **jouait** dans les vaudevilles militaires. Mais finalement, il **était entré** dans les chemins de fer et il ne le **regrettait** pas, parce que maintenant il **avait** une petite retraite. Il n'**avait** pas **été** heureux avec sa femme, mais dans l'ensemble, il s'**était** bien **habitué** à elle. Quand elle **était morte**, il s'**était senti** très seul. Alors, il **avait demandé** un chien à un camarade d'atelier et il **avait eu** celui-là très jeune. Il **avait fallu** le nourrir au biberon. Mais comme un chien vit moins qu'un homme, ils **avaient fini** par être vieux ensemble. ≪ Il **avait** mauvais caractère, m'a dit Salamano. De temps en temps, on **avait** des prises de bec. Mais c'**était** un bon chien quand même.≫

38 Le futur

38.1 Formation

A. General rule: The future tense is formed by adding to the infinitive of the verb the following endings:

je	parlerai	je	finirai
tu	parleras	tu	finiras
il	parlera	il	finira
nous	parlerons	nous	finirons
vous	parlerez	vous	finirez
ils	parleront	ils	finiront

B. Verbs ending in **-re** lose **e** before the ending of the future is added:

prendr¢	je prendrai
mettr¢	je mettrai
lir¢	je lirai
écrir¢	j'écrirai

C. Irregular future stems:

aller	j'**irai**
avoir	j'**aurai**
acquérir	j'**acquerrai**
s'asseoir	je m'**assiérai** *or* je m'**assoirai**
courir	je **courrai**
cueillir	je **cueillerai**
devoir	je **devrai**
envoyer	j'**enverrai**
être	je **serai**
faire	je **ferai**
falloir	il **faudra**
mourir	je **mourrai**
pleuvoir	il **pleuvra**
pouvoir	je **pourrai**
recevoir	je **recevrai**

savoir	je **saurai**
tenir	je **tiendrai**
valoir	je **vaudrai**
venir	je **viendrai**
voir	je **verrai**
vouloir	je **voudrai**

All verbs have the same stem in all persons. All verbs have the same regular endings.

38.2 Emploi

A. The future tense is used for actions expected to happen in the future.

B. It is used after **quand** if the action is in the future:

Quand je **serai** fatigué, j'irai me coucher.
When I am tired, I will go to bed.

C. After conjunctions of time, the future tense is used in French to express future actions. In English the present tense is used in this particular case. The most common conjunctions of time which may be followed by the **futur** or the **futur antérieur** are:

quand	*when*
lorsque	*when*
comme	*as*
tant que	*as long as*
après que	*after*
dès que	*as soon as*
aussitôt que	*as soon as*
pendant que	*while*
à mesure que	*as*

Aussitôt que vous **arriverez**, écrivez-moi.
As soon as you arrive, write me.
M'appellera-t-elle lorsqu'elle **sera** de retour?
Will she call me when she gets back?

38.3 Le future proche: **aller** + infinitif

The near future is formed with the present tense of the verb **aller** followed by an infinitive:

Je **vais écrire** une lettre.
Nous **allons étudier** toute la journée.

39 Le futur antérieur

39.1 Formation

The **futur antérieur** is formed with the future tense of the auxiliary verb and the past participle of the verb to be conjugated. Being a compound tense, the past participle will follow the usual patterns of agreement:

> J'**aurai fini** avant tout le monde.
> Elle **sera partie** avant six heures.
> Nous les **aurons lues** avant midi. (les leçons)

39.2 Emploi

The **futur antérieur** is used to indicate an action that will take place in the future before a specific moment or an action that will have taken place before another action in the future:

Nous **aurons terminé** notre devoir avant le dîner.
Aussitôt que j'**aurai vu** vos amis, je vous écrirai.
Lorsque j'**aurai pris** mon repas, je vous écouterai.
Nous regretterez-vous quand nous **serons partis**?
Il n'aura pas encore son diplôme quand vous **aurez** déjà **reçu** le vôtre.
Après qu'ils se **seront disputés**, ils se contenteront.

39.3 Idiomatic use of the future tenses: probability

> Ce **sera** un médecin.
> *He must be a doctor.*
> Ils l'**auront acheté** en Europe.
> *They must have bought it in Europe.*

40 Le conditionnel présent

40.1 Formation

A. General rule: The **conditionnel présent** is formed by adding to the infinitive the following endings:

je	parle**rais**	je	fini**rais**
tu	parle**rais**	tu	fini**rais**
il	parle**rait**	il	fini**rait**
nous	parle**rions**	nous	fini**rions**
vous	parle**riez**	vous	fini**riez**
ils	parle**raient**	ils	fini**raient**

B. Verbs ending in **-re** lose the **e** before the ending of the conditional is added:

prendr¢	je prend**rais**
mettr¢	je met**trais**
lir¢	je li**rais**
écrir¢	j'écri**rais**

C. The irregular conditional stems are identical with those of the future:

aller	j'**irais**
avoir	j'**aurais**
être	je **serais**
faire	je **ferais**

Note that the conditional endings are identical with the **imparfait** endings.

40.2 Emploi

The **conditionnel** is the mood used to express actions subject to a condition. The present conditional is used when this condition is not fulfilled at the present; the past conditional is used when this condition has not been fulfilled at a given moment in the past (see **phrases de condition** or if-clauses): Si j'étais riche, je **voyagerais**.

40.3 Idiomatic uses. The **conditionnel présent** is often used:

A. To express a polite request, statement, or wish:

> **Pourriez**-vous m'attendre un moment?
> Nous **aimerions** connaître votre opinion.
> **Voudriez**-vous avoir l'obligeance de me téléphoner?
> **Auriez**-vous la gentillesse de fermer cette porte?

B. To express hypothetical statements or questions:

> Ne **serait**-il pas plus sage d'arrêter de fumer?
> Michèle n'est pas venue; **serait**-elle malade?

C. To express actions that were considered future at a particular moment in the past:

> Il m'a dit qu'il **partirait** tôt.
> Je savais qu'elle ne m'**écouterait** pas.
> Je ne pensais pas que cela **finirait** ainsi!

41 Le conditionnel passé

41.1 Formation

The **conditionnel passé** is a compound tense. It is formed with the **conditionnel présent** of the auxiliary plus the past participle of the verb. The past participle follows the usual patterns of agreement:

> J'**aurais voulu** vous voir.
> Si nous avions réfléchi, nous n'**aurions** pas **fait** de fautes.
> Il ne l'**aurait** pas **vendue** si elle n'avait pas été en mauvais état.

41.2 Emploi

> The **conditionnel passé** is required when a condition has not been fulfilled at a given moment in the past:

> > Si j'avais été riche, j'**aurais voyagé**.

> The idiomatic uses are the same as for the **conditionnel présent**.

42 Les phrases de condition *(if-clauses)*

42 Les phrases de condition (if-clauses)

The most common conditional sentences involve the following sequences of tenses:

la condition (if-clause)	le résultat (result clause)
si + présent si + imparfait si + plus-que-parfait	futur conditionnel présent conditionnel passé

Si j'**ai** le temps, j'**irai** voir ce film.
Si elle **avait** le téléphone, je l'**appellerais**.
Si vous **aviez pris** l'avion du matin, vous **seriez arrivé** à temps.

A **si** clause may either precede or follow the result clause:

J'**irais** le voir si j'**avais** le temps.

43 L'impératif

A. The **impératif,** which has the function of expressing a command or a request, is composed of three forms derived from the present indicative *without* the subject pronouns:

tu parles	**parle**
nous parlons	**parlons**
vous parlez	**parlez**
tu finis	**finis**
nous finissons	**finissons**
vous finissez	**finissez**
tu vends	**vends**
nous vendons	**vendons**
vous vendez	**vendez**

The **-er** verbs (including **aller**) drop s except when followed by **y** or **en**:

Va à la maison.   but: **Vas-y**

B. Irregular imperatives:

avoir	**aie**	**avons**	**ayez**
être	**sois**	**soyons**	**soyez**
savoir	**sache**	**sachons**	**sachez**

C. The present subjunctive forms are used for the third-person command forms.

Qu'il **finisse.**	*Have him finish.*
Qu'elle **sorte** tout de suite!	*Have her leave now!*

The object pronouns are placed after the verb when used in an imperative sentence (see position of the **pronoms personnels**).

44 Le participe présent et le gérondif

44.1 Formation

The present participle is formed by substituting the ending -ant for the -ons of the first person plural, present indicative:

nous parlǿns̷	parlant
nous finissǿns̷	finissant
nous vendǿns̷	vendant
nous sortǿns̷	sortant

Irregular present participles:

avoir	**ayant**
être	**étant**
savoir	**sachant**

44.2 Emploi

Although the ending -ant of the **participe présent** is equivalent to the English -ing, the **participe présent** is never used in a progressive form (*I am speaking*). The present indicative is used instead: **je parle**.

A. The **participe présent** is used without the preposition **en**:

> Elle était assise, **buvant** son café.
> Je les ai vus, **parlant** au directeur.
> **Étant** malade, il n'a pu faire ce voyage.

Used verbally, the present participle is invariable.

B. Used as an adjective, the **participe présent** agrees in number and gender with the noun or pronoun it qualifies:

> des **films** amusant**s**
> une **femme** charmante
> un **examen** fatigant

44.3 Le gérondif = en + participe présent

The **gérondif** denotes that two actions take place simultaneously by the same person(s):

> Cet homme **fume en mangeant**.
> Il n'aime pas les ouvriers qui **parlent en travaillant**.
> Écoutez-vous la radio **en lisant** votre journal?
> Il est défendu de **boire** de la bière **en conduisant**.
> Il **s'est cassé** la jambe **en jouant** au football.
> Il m'**a raconté** cette histoire **en pleurant**.
> L'appétit **vient en mangeant**.

En is the only preposition that can be used with the **participe présent**. Other prepositions are followed by the infinitif (see the **infinitif**).

A few verbs have a **participe présent** that cannot be used as an adjective. A special adjective is then used instead with a variation in the spelling:

PARTICIPE	ADJECTIVE
sachant	savant
fatiguant	fatigant
pouvant	puissant
convainquant	convaincant
affluant	affluent
excellant	excellent
négligeant	négligent

45 L'infinitif

French verbs fall into three groups, which can be identified by the infinitive ending:

-er	1st group	(regular verbs)
-ir	2nd group	(regular verbs)
-ir, -oir, and **-re**	3rd group	(irregular verbs)

The infinitive expresses the meaning of the verb in a general way without distinction of person or number.

A. In French, the infinitive is used after all prepositions except **en** which takes the present participle:

> Il faut manger **pour vivre**.
> Il est temps **de partir**.
> Elle ne peut pas rester **sans fumer**.
> C'est **à prendre** ou **à laisser**.

B. After the preposition **après**, the **infinitif passé** must be used. The past infinitive is formed by the present infinitive of **avoir** or **être** and the past participle of the main verb:

> **Après avoir mangé**, ils sont allés au cinéma.
> **Après avoir fini** son devoir, il est sorti.
> **Après être arrivé** chez moi, je lui ai téléphoné.
> **Après s'être disputés**, ils se sont embrassés.

C. The preposition is repeated if there is more than one infinitive:

> Les étudiants apprennent **à** parler et **à** lire.
> Il a besoin **de** travailler, **d'**économiser et **d'**étudier.

D. The negative is formed by placing **ne pas** before the infinitive:

> Je regrette de **ne pas** avoir parlé.
> Je crains de **ne pas** pouvoir le faire.

E. In French, when two verbs are used consecutively, the second one is always an infinitive whether preceded or not by a preposition (see the following lists):

> Je **compte partir** demain.
> Il **parviendra à obtenir** son diplôme.
> Vous avez **oublié de lire** cet article.

45.1 Verbs directly followed by an infinitive without any preposition

aimer	*to like, to love*
aimer mieux	*to prefer*
aller	*to go*
avoir beau	*to be in vain*
avouer	*to confess, to admit*
compter	*to expect, to plan*
courir	*to run*
croire	*to believe, to think*
daigner	*to deign*
déclarer	*to declare*
descendre	*to descend, to go down*
désirer	*to desire, to wish*
devoir	*to have to, must, ought*
écouter	*to listen*
entendre	*to hear*
envoyer	*to send*
espérer	*to hope*
faillir[1]	*almost, nearly*
faire	*to make, to cause*
falloir[1]	*to be necessary*
s'imaginer	*to imagine*
juger	*to consider*
laisser	*to allow, to let*
oser	*to dare*
paraître	*to appear*
penser	*to think*
pouvoir	*to be able, may, can*
préférer	*to prefer*
prétendre	*to claim, to assert*
se rappeler	*to recall, to remember*
regarder	*to look at*
rentrer	*to return home*

[1] Used only in the third person singular.

retourner	to return
revenir	to come back
savoir	to know how to
sembler	to seem
sentir	to feel
souhaiter	to wish
supposer	to suppose
témoigner	to testify
valoir mieux	to be better
venir	to come
voir	to see
vouloir	to want, to wish

Examples:

Il **compte partir** demain.
Elles **souhaitent avoir** l'argent nécessaire.
Il **vaut mieux prévenir** que guérir.
Nous **préférons écouter** la musique classique.
Tu **prétends savoir** beaucoup de choses.
Je **pense prendre** l'avion pour aller à Paris.
Il **regarde voler** les oiseaux.
Nous **devrons marcher** toute la journée.
Il **faut réfléchir** avant de répondre.
Je **crois pouvoir** m'occuper de cette personne.

45.2 Verbs requiring à before a following infinitive

s'accoutumer à	to get accustomed to
aider à	to help
aimer (à *optional*)	to like to, to love to
s'amuser à	to enjoy, to have fun
s'appliquer à	to apply oneself to
apprendre à	to learn to
arriver à	to succeed in
s'attendre à	to expect to
autoriser à	to authorize to
avoir à	to have to, must
avoir de la peine à	to have difficulty
se borner à	to limit oneself to
chercher à	to seek to
commencer à	to begin to
consentir à	to consent to
consister à	to consist in

continuer à	*to continue to*
contribuer à	*to contribute to*
coopérer à	*to cooperate in*
se décider à	*to decide to*
demander à	*to ask to*
se dévouer à	*to devote oneself to*
se disposer à	*to get ready to*
encourager à	*to encourage to*
engager à	*to induce to*
s'engager à	*to pledge to*
enseigner à	*to teach to*
s'exercer à	*to practice*
exciter à	*to excite to*
se fatiguer à	*to tire oneself in*
forcer à	*to force*
s'habituer à	*to get used to*
hésiter à	*to hesitate to*
inviter à	*to invite to*
se mettre à	*to begin to*
obliger à	*to oblige to, to force to*
s'occuper à	*to be busy (at)*
s'offrir à	*to offer to*
parvenir à	*to succeed in*
penser à	*to consider*
persévérer à	*to persevere in*
persister à	*to persist in*
prendre plaisir à	*to take pleasure in*
se préparer à	*to prepare to, to get ready to*
renoncer à	*to renounce*
se résigner à	*to resign oneself to*
réussir à	*to succeed in*
servir à	*to serve to*
songer à	*to think of, to consider*
tarder à	*to delay in*
tendre à	*to tend to*
tenir à	*to be anxious to*
travailler à	*to work to*
viser à	*to aim to*

45.3 Verbs requiring **de** before a following infinitive

s'abstenir de	*to abstain from*
achever de	*to finish*

il s'agit de	it is a matter of
avertir de	to warn to
blâmer	to blame
cesser de	to cease to
charger de	to entrust with
se charger de	to take upon oneself
choisir de	to choose to
commander de	to order to
conseiller de	to advise to
se contenter de	to be content with
convaincre de	to convince to
convenir de	to agree to
craindre de	to fear to
décider de	to decide to
défendre de	to forbid to
demander de	to ask to
se dépêcher de	to hurry to
détester de	to detest to
dire de	to tell to
dispenser de	to exempt from
écrire de	to write to
s'efforcer de	to make an effort to
empêcher de	to prevent from
s'empresser de	to hasten to
s'ennuyer de	to be bored to
entreprendre de	to undertake to
essayer de	to try to
s'étonner de	to be surprised to
éviter de	to avoid
s'excuser de	to decline to, to excuse oneself for
exiger de	to demand
féliciter de	to congratulate on
finir de	to finish
être forcé de	to be forced to
se garder de	to take care not to
se hâter de	to hasten to
interdire de	to forbid to
jouir de	to enjoy to
jurer de	to swear to
manquer de	to fail to, to come near to
menacer de	to threaten to

mériter de	*to deserve to*
négliger de	*to neglect to*
notifier de	*to notify to*
être obligé de	*to have to, to be obliged to*
obtenir de	*to obtain*
s'occuper de	*to take care of*
offrir de	*to offer to*
ordonner de	*to order to*
oublier de	*to forget to*
pardonner de	*to pardon for*
permettre de	*to permit to*
persuader de	*to persuade to*
se plaindre de	*to complain of*
prendre garder de	*to be careful not to*
prendre l'habitude de	*to get into the habit of*
prendre la peine de	*to take the trouble to*
prendre soin de	*to be careful to*
presser de	*to urge to*
se presser de	*to hasten to*
prier de	*to beg to, to ask to*
se priver de	*to deprive oneself of*
promettre de	*to promise to*
proposer de	*to propose to*
recommander de	*to recommend to*
refuser de	*to refuse to*
regretter de	*to regret to*
se réjouir de	*to rejoice at*
remercier de	*to thank for*
se repentir de	*to repent*
reprocher de	*to reproach for*
rire de	*to laugh about*
risquer de	*to risk*
souffrir de	*to suffer about*
soupçonner de	*to suspect of*
sourire de	*to smile about*
se souvenir de	*to remember*
suggérer de	*to suggest to*
tâcher de	*to try to, to attempt to*
tenter de	*to try to, to attempt to*
se vanter de	*to boast about*
venir de	*to have just*

45.4 Verbs requiring a preposition before a noun in English and none in French

regarder	*to look at*
demander	*to ask for*
approuver	*to approve of*
rencontrer	*to meet with*
attendre	*to wait for*
payer	*to pay for*
souhaiter	*to wish for*
écouter	*to listen to*
chercher	*to look for*
espérer	*to hope for*

45.5 Verbs requiring a preposition before a noun in French and none in English

répondre à	*to answer*
résister à	*to resist*
enseigner à (*for persons only*)	*to teach*
succéder à	*to succeed*
reprocher à (*for persons only*)	*to reproach*
nuire à	*to harm*
renoncer à	*to renounce*
pardonner à (*for persons only*)	*to forgive*
désobéir à	*to disobey*
obéir à	*to obey*
se fier à	*to trust*
ressembler à	*to resemble*
plaire à	*to please*
persuader à	*to persuade*
jouer à	*to play (sports, games)*
se souvenir de	*to remember*
se méfier de	*to distrust*
se douter de	*to suspect*
s'apercevoir de	*to notice*
avoir besoin de	*to need*
jouir de	*to enjoy*
se rendre compte de	*to realize*
jouer de	*to play (instruments)*
se marier avec	*to marry*
entrer dans	*to enter*
téléphoner à (*for persons only*)	*to telephone*

46 Les verbes pronominaux
(reflexive verbs)

46.1 Formation

In French, all verbs taking a direct or an indirect object can be turned into reflexive verbs by using a special object pronoun called **pronom réfléchi**:

Je	**me**	lave	et	je	**m'**	habille.
Tu	**te**	laves	et	tu	**t'**	habilles.
Il	**se**	lave	et	il	**s'**	habille.
Nous	**nous**	lavons	et	nous	**nous**	habillons.
Vous	**vous**	lavez	et	vous	**vous**	habillez.
Ils	**se**	lavent	et	ils	**s'**	habillent.

The **pronom réfléchi** is always placed before the verb in a simple tense or before the auxiliary in a compound tense, except in the **impératif affirmatif**:

Je **me** rase tous les matins.
Elle ne **se** maquille pas quand elle reste chez elle.
Nous **nous** sommes écrit pendant les vacances.
but:
Asseyez-**vous**.   Arrête-**toi**.

Note that **te (t')** becomes **toi** in the **impératif affirmatif**. The **pronom réfléchi** is always in the same person as the subject even if the infinitive form of the verb is used:

Je ne désire pas **me** coucher trop tôt.
Il n'a pas eu le temps de **se** peigner ce matin.
Vous n'aurez pas le temps de **vous** reposer.

The **verbes pronominaux** are all conjugated with the auxiliary verb **être**.

46.2 Accord du participe passé (*agreement of the past participle*)

The **verbes pronominaux** can be divided into four categories:

A. **Réfléchis**

The subject carries out an action on itself:

Je me suis lavé avant le petit déjeuner.
Elle s'est coiffée avant son rendez-vous.

[121]

Il **s'est coupé** en se rasant.
Je me serais arrêté à temps, si j'avais su.

B. Réciproques

A reciprocal verb expresses an action done by two or more agents, one upon the other:

Nous nous connaissons depuis longtemps.
Ils s'embrassent en public.
Colette et Alain ne **se parlent** pas.
Ils ne **s'écrivent** pas, **ils se voient** tous les jours.

C. Verbes pronominaux à sens idiomatique

Some verbs, when used in their pronominal form, have a different meaning:

se coucher	*to go to bed*
s'en aller	*to leave, to go away*
s'amuser	*to have fun*
se douter	*to suspect*
se contenir	*to restrain oneself*
s'endormir	*to fall asleep*

See the following list for more verbs.

D. Verbes essentiellement pronominaux

These verbs do not exist in their nonpronominal form:

se suicider	*to commit suicide*
se méfier de	*to distrust*
s'enfuir	*to flee*

See the following list.

E. All verbs falling into categories A and B (**réfléchis** and **réciproques**), when used in compound tenses, follow the same rule as verbs using the auxiliary **avoir**. The past participle must agree in gender and in number with the *direct object* if it *precedes* the verb. The **pronom réfléchi** is usually the preceding direct object:

Elles **se** sont lavées. (**Se** is the direct object).
Elles se sont lavé **les mains**. (No agreement: the direct object follows).
Elles **se** sont écrit. (**Se** is the indirect object).

F. All verbs falling into categories C and D follow the rule for other verbs using the auxiliary **être**. The past participle must agree with the *subject*:

Elles se sont disputées.
Ils s'étaient abstenus.

Often a pronominal form replaces a sentence with **on**. The direct object becomes the subject of the verb:

On paye cher les abus.
Les abus **se payent** cher.

46.3 Liste des verbes essentiellement pronominaux

s'accouder	*to lean on one's elbow(s)*
s'absenter	*to absent oneself*
s'abstenir	*to abstain*
s'adonner	*to devote oneself to*
s'affairer	*to busy oneself with*
s'affaisser	*to collapse*
s'agenouiller	*to kneel*
s'arroger	*to assume a right*
s'attabler	*to sit at a table*
s'avachir	*to become slack, sloppy*
se bagarrer	*to have a fight, a scuffle*
se blottir	*to crouch*
se cabrer	*to buck*
se démener	*to strive hard*
s'ébattre	*to frolic*
s'écrier	*to exclaim, to cry out*
s'écrouler	*to crumble, to collapse*
s'efforcer	*to make an effort*
s'emparer de	*to take possession of*
s'empresser de	*to hasten to*
s'enfuir	*to flee*
s'enquérir	*to inquire*
s'envoler	*to fly away*
s'évader	*to escape*
s'évanouir	*to faint*
s'evertuer	*to exert oneself*
s'exclamer	*to exclaim*
s'extasier	*to be in ecstasy over . . .*
se gargariser	*to gargle*
s'ingénier	*to exercise one's wits*
se lamenter	*to lament*
se méfier de	*to distrust*

se méprendre	*to be mistaken*
se moquer de	*to make fun of*
s'obstiner à	*to be obstinate, to persist*
se prosterner	*to prostrate oneself*
se rebeller	*to revolt*
se récrier	*to exclaim, to cry out*
se réfugier	*to take refuge*
se repentir de	*to repent, to regret*
se soucier de	*to concern oneself about*
se souvenir de	*to remember*
se suicider	*to commit suicide*

46.4 Quelques verbes pronominaux à sens idiomatique

s'entendre	*to get along*	entendre	*to hear*
se passer	*to happen*	passer	*to pass*
se mettre à	*to begin*	mettre	*to put*
se servir de	*to make use of*	servir	*to serve*
se disputer	*to quarrel*	disputer	*to dispute*
se tromper	*to make a mistake*	tromper	*to fool*
s'occuper de	*to busy oneself with*	occuper	*to occupy*
se dépêcher	*to hurry*	dépêcher	*to dispatch*
se faire à	*to get used to*	faire	*to do, to make*
se plaindre	*to complain*	plaindre	*to pity*
s'ennuyer	*to be bored*	ennuyer	*to annoy*
s'appeler	*to be called*	appeler	*to call*

47 Le discours indirect

A. When you relate a statement or a dialogue without quoting the exact words, you use indirect discourse.

1. To relate a sentence expressing a command or an order, replace the imperative form by **de** + infinitive:

Le professeur:— **Finissez** la lecture.
Indirect discourse: Le professeur nous dit **de finir** la lecture.
Ma mère me dit:—Ferme la porte.
Indirect discourse: Ma mère me dit **de fermer** la porte.

2. To relate a sentence expressing a statement or a fact, use **que** + conjugated verb:

Robert:—Je suis content de mon travail.
Robert dit **qu'il est** content de son travail.

3. To relate an interrogative sentence, **est-ce que?** becomes **si** + conjugated verb:

—Est-ce que vous écrivez?   Il me demande **si j'écris.**

Inversion without an interrogative word becomes **si** + conjugated verb:

—Ecrivez-vous à votre mère?
Il me demande **si j'écris** à ma mère.
—Est-ce un bon livre?
Il me demande **si c'est** un bon livre.

Qu'est-ce que? and **que?** become **ce que** + conjugated verb:

—Qu'est-ce que vous faites?   —Que faites-vous?
Il nous demande **ce que** nous faisons.

Qu'est-ce qui? becomes **ce qui**:

—Qu'est-ce qui est difficile?
Il veut savoir **ce qui** est difficile.

Qui? and **qui est-ce qui?** become **qui** + conjugated verb:

—**Qui est-ce qui** va au cinéma?   —**Qui** va au cinéma?
Il demande **qui** va au cinéma.

The other interrogative words do not change, but they must be repeated in indirect discourse:

> –Combien d'argent avez-vous?
> Il me demande **combien** d'argent j'ai.
> –Quelle est votre profession?
> Il veut savoir **quelle** est ma profession.
> –Pourquoi partez-vous?
> Il désire savoir **pourquoi** nous partons.

B. **Concordance des temps** (Sequence of tenses)

1. If the verb in direct discourse is in the **présent**, this tense has to be replaced by the **imparfait** in indirect discourse when it is introduced by a verb in the past tense:

> –Vos compositions **sont** excellentes.
> Il a dit que nos compositions **étaient** excellentes.

Il a dit shows that you are relating something that happened in the past; therefore **sont** becomes **étaient**. Following the same pattern:

VERB IN DIRECT DISCOURSE		VERB IN INDIRECT DISCOURSE
présent	becomes	**imparfait**
passé composé	becomes	**plus-que-parfait**
futur	becomes	**conditionnel présent**
imparfait	stays	**imparfait**

The other tenses do not change.

2. The sequence of tenses applies to any compound sentence in French. When the verb in the main clause is in the present indicative, the verb in the subordinate clause conveying a chronological relationship must be changed if the verb in the principal clause is changed to a past tense:

Je **pense** que Georges **a** envie d'une voiture. (présent)
Je **pensais** que Georges **avait** envie d'une voiture. (imparfait)

Elle me **dit** qu'elle **a oublié** ses clés. (passé composé)
Elle m'**a dit** qu'elle **avait oublié** ses clés. (plus-que-parfait)

Nous **sommes** certains qu'ils **passeront** de bonnes vacances. (futur)
Nous **étions certains** qu'ils **passeraient** de bonnes vacances. (conditionnel présent)

C. Other changes which occur in indirect discourse

Adjectives and pronouns:

   —Je **vous** prête **ma** voiture.
   Il m'a dit qu'il **me** prêtait **sa** voiture.

Expressions of time

aujourd'hui	becomes	**ce jour-là**
demain	becomes	**le lendemain**
après-demain	becomes	**le surlendemain**
hier	becomes	**la veille**
avant-hier	becomes	**l'avant-veille**
ici	becomes	**là**
en ce moment	becomes	**à ce moment-là**

To the other expressions of time, add **là (ce matin-là, ce jour-là**, etc). **Lundi prochain** becomes **le lundi suivant**, **la semaine prochaine** becomes **la semaine suivante**, etc.

D. Useful verbs to express indirect discourse.

ajouter	crier	indiquer
avouer	chuchoter	objecter
affirmer	dire	insinuer
assurer	demander	insister
annoncer	répondre	expliquer
avertir	répéter	suggérer
constater	déclarer	

There is no inversion in indirect discourse.

48 La forme passive

The passive voice is formed with the auxiliary verb **être** and the past participle of a verb that takes a direct object (verbe transitif direct). The past participle must agree in number and gender with the subject. Any tense may be used:

FORME ACTIVE: Le professeur (sujet) **corrige** (forme active) les devoirs (objet direct)

FORMES PASSIVES:

Les devoirs (sujet) **sont corrigés** (forme passive) par le professeur (agent).
Les devoirs **étaient corrigés** par le professeur.
Les devoirs **ont été corrigés** par le professeur.
Les devoirs **furent corrigés** par le professeur.
Les devoirs **avaient été corrigés** par le professeur.
Les devoirs **seront corrigés** par le professeur.
Les devoirs **seraient corrigés** par le professeur.
Les devoirs **auront été corrigés** par le professeur.
Les devoirs **auraient été corrigés** par le professeur.
Il faut que les devoirs **soient corrigés** par le professeur.
Je doute que les devoirs **aient été corrigés** par le professeur.

The direct object in the active version becomes the subject in the passive, while the subject becomes the agent, usually introduced by the preposition **par**. Sometimes the agent is indicated by the preposition **de** with verbs denoting emotion:

Jacqueline **est adorée de** tout le monde.

or with the verbs **accompagner, suivre, couvrir, assister,** and others:

Les enfants **sont accompagnés de** leurs parents.
Les montagnes **sont couvertes de** neige.

When the subject in the active voice is **on**, no agent is expressed in the passive voice:

On a volé notre auto.   Notre auto a été volée.

49 Expressions of time and duration

A. **depuis** and **depuis que** (*since*)

To express an action or condition which started in the past and is still going on, **depuis** or **depuis que** is used with a verb in the **présent**:

> Nous **habitons** Los Angeles **depuis cinq ans**.
> **Depuis qu'elle est** ici, elle se sent mieux.

Depuis is used with the **imparfait** to express an action which started in the past and has continued until a specific moment in the past:

Je **travaillais depuis deux ans** dans cette compagnie quand j'ai perdu ma place.
Depuis que nous étions en vacances, il ne faisait que pleuvoir.

Depuis is always followed by a noun or an expression of time.
Depuis que is followed by a verb.

B. **il y a** + time expression and **il y a . . . que**

il y a + time expression means *ago*.

> J'ai reçu mon diplôme **il y a trois ans**.

il y a . . . que Between **il y a** and **que** an expression of time must be used. It has the same meaning as **depuis** + time expression:

> **Il y a cinq ans que** nous habitons Los Angeles.
> **Il y avait cinq ans que** nous habitions Los Angeles.

C. **Voici . . . que** and **voilà . . . que** are used the same way as **il y a . . . que**:

> **Voici (voilà) cinq ans que** nous habitons Los Angeles.

D. **Pendant** (*during*) and **pendant que** (*while*) may be used with verbs in any tense:

> Je l'interrogerai **pendant le dîner**.
> **Pendant qu'elle regardait** la télévision, il lisait.

Pendant is always followed by a noun or an expression of time.
Pendant que is followed by a verb.

50 Le subjonctif présent

50.1 Formation

A. The stem of the **subjonctif présent** for all regular verbs and most irregular verbs is obtained by dropping the **-ent** ending of the third person plural of the **indicatif présent** and adding the following endings:

ils parl~~ent~~	que je	parle
	que tu	parles
	qu'il	parle
	que nous	parlions
	que vous	parliez
	qu'ils	parlent
ils finiss~~ent~~	que je	finisse
	que tu	finisses
	qu'il	finisse
	que nous	finissions
	que vous	finissiez
	qu'ils	finissent
ils vend~~ent~~	que je	vende
ils boiv~~ent~~	que je	boive
ils prenn~~ent~~	que je	prenne

B. Verbs which have a change of stem in the first and second persons plural in the **présent indicatif** will have the same change in the **subjonctif présent**:

que je prenne	que nous **pren**ions, que vous **pren**iez
que je boive	que nous **buv**ions, que vous **buv**iez
que je reçoive	que nous **recev**ions, que vous **recev**iez

C. The following verbs have a special stem:

faire	**fass-**	que je fasse, etc. . . .
pouvoir	**puiss-**	que je puisse, etc. . . .
savoir	**sach-**	que je sache, etc. . . .

[130]

D. The following verbs change stems in the conjugation:

aller	que j'	**aille**	que nous	allions
	que tu	**ailles**	que vous	alliez
	qu'il	**aille**	qu'ils	**aillent**

vouloir	que je	**veuille**	que nous	voulions
	que tu	**veuilles**	que vous	vouliez
	qu'il	**veuille**	qu'ils	**veuillent**

valoir	que je	**vaille**	que nous	valions
	que tu	**vailles**	que vous	valiez
	qu'il	**vaille**	qu'ils	**vaillent**

E. Irregular impersonal verbs

falloir	(il faut)	qu'il **faille**
pleuvoir	(il pleut)	qu'il **pleuve**

F. The verbs **avoir** and **être** have irregular stems and are the *only* verbs to have irregular endings:

avoir	que j'**aie**	que nous **ayons**
	que tu **aies**	que vous **ayez**
	qu'il **ait**	qu'ils **aient**

être	que je **sois**	que nous **soyons**
	que tu **sois**	que vous **soyez**
	qu'il **soit**	qu'ils **soient**

50.2 Emploi

The subjunctive is the mood of possibility. It never presents an action or a state as a fact. The subjunctive is used almost exclusively in subordinate clauses introduced by **que**, which may never be omitted. The use of a subjunctive in a subordinate clause depends upon the idea expressed in the main clause.

The **subjonctif présent** is used when the action expressed by the subordinate verb is simultaneous with the action of the main verb or future to the action of the main verb.

The subjunctive occurs in the subordinate clause when the verb in the main clause expresses:

A. doubt or uncertainty:

> Je **doute** qu'elle **vienne** ce soir.

Il **n'est pas sûr** que nous **réussissions**.
Il **est possible** que le professeur **soit** malade.

B. desire, command, or prohibition:

Je **veux** que vous **sortiez** immédiatement.
Sa famille **voudrait** qu'il **aille** à l'université.
Il **exige** que nous **soyons** à temps.

C. necessity:

Il **faut** que vous **sachiez** la vérité.
Il **est nécessaire** que vous vous **mettiez** à étudier.
Il **est indispensable** que j'**aille** à la poste.

D. an emotion or a personal feeling (joy, sorrow, fear, etc.):

Je **regrette** que vous ne **puissiez** venir avec nous.
J'ai peur qu'il ne **fasse** très froid cet hiver.

50.3 The subjunctive is required

A. when the antecedent of a relative pronoun is uncertain or nonexistent:

Je cherche un hotel qui ne **soit** pas trop loin.
Il n'a pas d'amis qui lui **soit** fidèle.
Il n'y a pas de femme qui **soit** parfaite.

B. when the antecedent is a superlative or after the expressions **le seul, l'unique,
le premier, le dernier**:

C'est **le seul médicament** qui **puisse** le sauver.
Paris est **la plus belle ville** que je **connaisse**.
C'est **l'unique personne** que je **craigne**.

C. after certain conjunctions (see conjunctions):

Il prendra l'avion **bien qu'il n'ait** pas l'argent.
Pourvu qu'ils soient à l'heure.
Je l'ai fait **sans que vous** me le **demandiez**.
Elle a téléphoné **pour que vous** l'**invitiez**.
Nous nous parlons **quoique nous soyons** ennemis.
J'irai voir ce film **à moins qu'il n'y ait** plus de places.
J'attendrai **jusqu'à ce que vous changiez** d'avis.

D. in clauses introduced by *whoever, whatever, wherever, no matter what, no matter how,* etc.:

Qui que vous **soyez**	*whoever*
Quoi que vous **fassiez**	*no matter what*
Quelques raisons **que** vous **ayez**	*whatever*

Also: **quel . . . que, quels . . . que, quelle . . . que,** etc.

E. in main clauses to express an order in the third person singular or plural:

> **Qu'ils s'en aillent!**
> **Qu'il prenne** l'autobus!

F. in idiomatic expressions:

Soit!	*So be it.*
Vive la paix!	*Let us have peace!*
Que Dieu vous bénisse!	*May God bless you!*
Grand bien vous fasse!	*Much good may it do you!*

50.4 The subjunctive is not used

A. when the verb in the main clause expresses a certainty; the indicative is used for all tenses:

> Je **suis certain** qu'ils **viendront**.
> Le professeur **dit** que je **fais** beaucoup de fautes.
> Elle **sait** que je lui **ai téléphoné**.
> Il **est évident** que les journaux ne **disent** pas tout.

B. after verbs expressing an opinion such as **penser, croire, supposer, s'imaginer, trouver, espérer,** and others in an affirmative sentence. Because of the implication of doubt, these verbs are followed by the subjunctive in a negative or an interrogative sentence:

> Je **pense** que son frère **est** malade.
> Je **ne pense pas** que son frère **soit** malade.
> Je **crois** qu'elle **viendra**.
> **Croyez-vous** qu'elle **vienne**?

C. after **il est probable**. The indicative is used:

> Il **est probable** que nous **aurons** un examen.

but:

Il **est peu probable** que nous **ayons** un examen.

D. after conjunctions such as **pendant que, parce que, ainsi que**, etc. (see conjunctions). The indicative is used:

Il s'amusait **pendant qu'elle travaillait.**
Vous avez réussi **parce que vous avez étudié.**

E. when the subject is the same in the main clause and in the subordinate clause. The infinitive must be used. Some verbs require a preposition before the infinitive (see the infinitive):

Mon père **préfère savoir** la vérité.
but:
Je préfère que mon père **sache** la vérité.

Il **craint d'arriver** en retard.
but:
Il craint que nous **arrivions** en retard.

51 Le subjonctif passé

51.1 Formation

The **subjonctif passé** is formed with the auxiliary verb in the **subjonctif présent** plus the past participle of the verb:

> que j'**aie parlé**
> qu'il **soit parti**

51.2 Emploi

All the rules for the **subjonctif présent** apply, except that the action of the subordinate verb is already completed at the time expressed by the main verb:

> Je doute qu'il **ait téléphoné** ce matin.
> Il est possible que nous nous **soyons trompés**.

52

Verbs requiring the subjunctive

accepter (de)
aimer
aimer mieux
approuver
attendre (de)
avoir besoin (de)
avoir envie (de)
avoir hâte (de)
avoir honte (de)
avoir peur (de)
commander (de)
conjurer (de)
consentir (à)
craindre (de)
défendre (de)
demander (de)
déplorer
désapprouver
désespérer (de)
désirer
douter (de)
écrire (de)
empêcher (de)
s'étonner (de)
être affligé (de)
être bien aise (de)
être charmé (de)
être content (de)
être désolé (de)
être enchanté (de)

être étonné (de)
être fâché (de)
être fier (de)
être heureux (de)
être indigné (de)
être mécontent (de)
être ravi (de)
être satisfait (de)
être triste (de)
éviter (de)
exiger (de)
se fâcher (de)
s'opposer à ce que
ordonner (de)
permettre (de)
se plaindre (de)
préférer
prendre garde
prier (de)
regretter (de)
se réjouir (de)
souhaiter
supplier (de)
tenir à ce que
trouver bon (de)
trouver injuste (de)
trouver juste (de)
trouver naturel (de)
vouloir

53 Impersonal expressions requiring the subjunctive

c'est dommage (de)
c'est honteux (de)
c'est peu probable (de)
c'est une honte (de)
il convient (de)
il est à désirer (de)
il est bon (de)
il est contestable (de)
il est convenable (de)
il est curieux (de)
il est dommage (de)
il est douteux (de)
il est essentiel (de)
il est fâcheux (de)
il est faux (de)
il est heureux (de)
il est important (de)
il est impossible (de)
il est indispensable (de)
il est injuste (de)
il est juste (de)
il est mauvais (de)

il est naturel (de)
il est nécessaire (de)
il est peu probable (de)
il est possible (de)
il est préférable (de)
il est rare (de)
il est regrettable (de)
il est temps (de)
il est urgent (de)
il est utile (de)
il faut
il importe (de)
il n'est pas certain (de)
il n'est pas clair (de)
il n'est pas évident (de)
il n'est pas sûr (de)
il n'est pas vrai (de)
il semble
il se peut
il suffit (de)
il vaut mieux

Use **de** instead of **que** before an infinitive.

An impersonal expression followed by an infinitive conveys a very general meaning.

54

Le verbe causatif:
faire + infinitif

When followed by an infinitive, **faire** is causative, that is, the subject of the verb causes an action to be done by another person:

> Le professeur a **fait lire** la leçon par les étudiants.

The past participle of causative **faire** is invariable:

> La leçon qu'il a **fait** lire. (no agreement)

Object pronouns precede the verb **faire** and not the infinitive, except in the **impératif affirmatif**:

> Il **les** a fait travailler.
> Il ne **la lui** fait pas lire.
> but:
> Faites-**les** travailler.

Idiomatic expressions with faire

Il fait beau.	*The weather is fine.*
Il fait mauvais.	*The weather is bad.*
Il fait chaud.	*It is warm.*
Il fait froid.	*It is cold.*
Il fait frais.	*It is cool.*
Il fait doux.	*It is mild.*
Il fait lourd.	*It is sultry.*
Il fait sec.	*It is dry.*
Il fait humide.	*It is humid.*
Il fait bon.	*It is nice.*
Il fait du vent.	*It is windy.*
Il fait du soleil.	*It is sunny.*
Il fait jour.	*It is daylight.*
Il fait nuit.	*It is dark (at night).*
Il fait noir.	*It is dark (at night).*
Il fait sombre.	*It is dark (in daytime).*
Il fait clair.	*It is clear.*
Il se fait tard.	*It is getting late.*
Il fait glissant.	*It is slippery.*
Il fait de l'orage.	*It is stormy.*
Il fait brumeux.	*It is misty.*

but:

Il pleuvine.	*It drizzles.*
Il neige.	*It is snowing.*
Il pleut.	*It is raining.*
Il tonne.	*It is thundering.*
Il gèle.	*It is freezing.*
Il grêle.	*It is hailing.*
Il bruine.	*It is drizzling.*
Il y a de la boue.	*It is muddy.*
Il y a des éclairs.	*It is lightening.*
Il y a une brise.	*There is a breeze.*

faire attention	*to pay attention*
faire semblant	*to pretend*
faire une promenade	*to take a walk*
faire des excuses	*to apologize*
faire des adieux	*to say good-bye*
se faire faire	*to have something done for oneself*
faire un faux pas	*to make a blunder*
faire la cour	*to court*
Cela ne fait rien.	*It does not matter.*
faire sa toilette	*to groom oneself*
faire partie d'un club	*to belong to a club*
faire le tour de	*to go around*
se faire mal à	*to hurt (something)*

56   Le verbe <u>devoir</u>

The basic meaning of the verb **devoir** is *to owe*:

> Je **dois** dix dollars à mon frère.
> Si nous achetons cette voiture, nous **devrons** beaucoup d'argent.

When followed by an infinitive, the verb **devoir** has various meanings according to tense and context:

1. must, have to

> Je **dois** terminer ce travail ce soir.
> On **doit** être fidèle.

2. ought to, should

> Nous **devrions** être de retour avant minuit.
> Vous **devriez** faire ce travail plus vite.

3. had to

> Ils **ont dû** faire la queue au cinéma.
> Nous **avons dû** attendre longtemps.

4. probability, must be, must have

> Elle n'est pas venue, elle **doit** être malade.
> Je suis arrivé en retard, elle **a dû** être fâchée.

5. In the **imparfait,** it denotes a repeated obligation in the past or an action that did not materialize:

> Quand j'étais petit, je **devais** me lever à six heures tous les jours.
> Il **devait** recevoir son diplôme l'été passé.

57

Les verbes connaître et savoir

A. **Connaître** means *to be acquainted with* a person or a thing (a city, a movie, a book, a story, a play, etc.):

> Je ne **connais** pas la Chine.
> **Connaissez**-vous mon père?
> Il **connaît** très bien le chemin.

B. **Savoir** means *to know* intellectually, to possess knowledge; hence it can never be used with a person:

> **Savez**-vous jouer de la guitare?
> Je ne **sais** pas le japonais.

Savoir + infinitif means to know how.

> Elle **sait** très bien **cuisiner**.

Tables of irregular verbs (third group)

INFINITIF		INDICATIF			
PARTICIPES		PRÉSENT	FUTUR	IMPARFAIT	PASSÉ SIMPLE
acquérir	j'	acquiers	acquerrai	acquérais	acquis
to acquire	tu	acquiers	acquerras	acquérais	acquis
acquérant	il	acquiert	acquerra	acquérait	acquit
acquis	nous	acquérons	acquerrons	acquérions	acquîmes
	vous	acquérez	acquerrez	acquériez	acquîtes
	ils	acquièrent	acquerront	acquéraient	acquirent
aller	je	vais	irai	allais	allai
to go	tu	vas	iras	allais	allas
allant	il	va	ira	allait	alla
allé	nous	allons	irons	allions	allâmes
	vous	allez	irez	alliez	allâtes
	ils	vont	iront	allaient	allèrent
assaillir	j'	assaille	assaillirai	assaillais	assaillis
to assault	tu	assailles	assailliras	assaillais	assaillis
to assail	il	assaille	assaillira	assaillait	assaillit
assaillant	nous	assaillons	assaillirons	assaillions	assaillîmes
assailli	vous	assaillez	assaillirez	assailliez	assaillîtes
	ils	assaillent	assailliront	assaillaient	assaillirent

58

Tables of irregular verbs (third group)

INFINITIF		INDICATIF			
PARTICIPES		PRÉSENT	FUTUR	IMPARFAIT	PASSÉ SIMPLE
acquérir	j'	acquiers	acquerrai	acquérais	acquis
to acquire	tu	acquiers	acquerras	acquérais	acquis
acquérant	il	acquiert	acquerra	acquérait	acquit
acquis	nous	acquérons	acquerrons	acquérions	acquîmes
	vous	acquérez	acquerrez	acquériez	acquîtes
	ils	acquièrent	acquerront	acquéraient	acquirent
aller	je	vais	irai	allais	allai
to go	tu	vas	iras	allais	allas
allant	il	va	ira	allait	alla
allé	nous	allons	irons	allions	allâmes
	vous	allez	irez	alliez	allâtes
	ils	vont	iront	allaient	allèrent
assaillir	j'	assaille	assaillirai	assaillais	assaillis
to assault	tu	assailles	assailliras	assaillais	assaillis
to assail	il	assaille	assaillira	assaillait	assaillit
assaillant	nous	assaillons	assaillirons	assaillions	assaillîmes
assailli	vous	assaillez	assaillirez	assailliez	assaillîtes
	ils	assaillent	assailliront	assaillaient	assaillirent

CONDITIONNEL	IMPÉRATIF	SUBJONCTIF	
		PRÉSENT	IMPARFAIT
acquerrais		acquière	acquisse
acquerrais	acquiers	acquières	acquisses
acquerrait		acquière	acquît
acquerrions	acquérons	acquérions	acquissions
acquerriez	acquérez	acquériez	acquissiez
acquerraient		acquièrent	acquissent
irais		aille	allasse
irais	va	ailles	allasses
irait		aille	allât
irions	allons	allions	allassions
iriez	allez	alliez	allassiez
iraient		aillent	allassent
assaillirais		assaille	assaillisse
assaillirais	assaille	assailles	assaillisses
assaillirait		assaille	assaillît
assaillirions	assaillons	assaillions	assaillissions
assailliriez	assaillez	assailliez	assaillissiez
assailliraient		assaillent	assaillissent

INFINITIF		INDICATIF			
PARTICIPES		PRÉSENT	FUTUR	IMPARFAIT	PASSÉ SIMPLE
asseoir	j'	assieds	assiérai	asseyais	assis
to seat	tu	assieds	assiéras	asseyais	assis
asseyant	il	assied	assiéra	asseyait	assit
assis	nous	asseyons	assiérons	asseyions	assîmes
	vous	asseyez	assiérez	asseyiez	assîtes
	ils	asseyent	assiéront	asseyaient	assirent
	or				
assoyant	j'	assois	assoirai	assoyais	
	tu	assois	assoiras	assoyais	
	il	assoit	assoira	assoyait	
	nous	assoyons	assoirons	assoyions	
	vous	assoyez	assoirez	assoyiez	
	ils	assoient	assoiront	assoyaient	
battre	je	bats	battrai	battais	battis
to beat	tu	bats	battras	battais	battis
battant	il	bat	battra	battait	battit
battu	nous	battons	battrons	battions	battîmes
	vous	battez	battrez	battiez	battîtes
	ils	battent	battront	battaient	battirent
boire	je	bois	boirai	buvais	bus
to drink	tu	bois	boiras	buvais	bus
buvant	il	boit	boira	buvait	but
bu	nous	buvons	boirons	buvions	bûmes
	vous	buvez	boirez	buviez	bûtes
	ils	boivent	boiront	buvient	burent
bouillir	je	bous	bouillirai	bouillais	bouillis
to boil	tu	bous	bouilliras	bouillais	bouillis
bouillant	il	bout	bouillira	bouillait	bouillit
bouilli	nous	bouillons	bouillirons	bouillions	bouillîmes
	vous	bouillez	bouillirez	bouilliez	bouillîtes
	ils	bouillent	bouilliront	bouillaient	bouillirent
conclure	je	conclus	conclurai	concluais	conclus
to conclude	tu	conclus	concluras	concluais	conclus
concluant	il	conclut	conclura	concluait	conclut
conclu	nous	concluons	conclurons	concluions	conclûmes
	vous	concluez	conclurez	concluiez	conclûtes
	ils	concluent	concluront	concluaient	conclurent

CONDITIONNEL	IMPÉRATIF	SUBJONCTIF	
		PRÉSENT	IMPARFAIT
assiérais		asseye	assisse
assiérais	assieds	asseyes	assisses
assiérait		asseye	assît
assiérions	asseyons	asseyions	assissions
assiériez	asseyez	asseyiez	assissiez
assiéraient		asseyent	assissent
or			
assoirais		assoie	
assoirais	assois	assoies	
assoirait		assoie	
assoirions	assoyons	assoyions	
assoiriez	assoyez	assoyiez	
assoiraient		assoient	
battrais		batte	battisse
battrais	bats	battes	batisses
battrait		batte	battît
battrions	battons	battions	battissions
battriez	battez	battiez	battissiez
battraient		battent	battissent
boirais		boive	busse
boirais	bois	boives	busses
boirait		boive	bût
boirions	buvons	buvions	bussions
boiriez	buvez	buviez	bussiez
boiraient		boivent	bussent
bouillirais		bouille	bouillisse
bouillirais	bous	bouilles	bouillisses
bouillirait		bouille	bouillît
bouillirions	bouillons	bouillions	bouillissions
bouilliriez	bouillez	bouilliez	bouillissiez
bouilliraient		bouillent	bouillissent
conclurais		conclue	conclusse
conclurais	conclus	conclues	conclusses
conclurait		conclue	conclût
conclurions	concluons	concluions	conclussions
concluriez	concluez	concluiez	conclussiez
concluraient		concluent	conclussent

INFINITIF		INDICATIF			
PARTICIPES		PRÉSENT	FUTUR	IMPARFAIT	PASSÉ SIMPLE
conduire	je	conduis	conduirai	conduisais	conduisis
to lead	tu	conduis	conduiras	conduisais	conduisis
to conduct	il	conduit	conduira	conduisait	conduisit
conduisant	nous	conduisons	conduirons	conduisions	conduisîmes
conduit	vous	conduisez	conduirez	conduisiez	conduisîtes
	ils	conduisent	conduiront	conduisaient	conduisirent
connaître	je	connais	connaîtrai	connaissais	connus
to know	tu	connais	connaîtras	connaissais	connus
connaissant	il	connaît	connaîtra	connaissait	connut
connu	nous	connaissons	connaîtrons	connaissions	connûmes
	vous	connaissez	connaîtrez	connaissiez	connûtes
	ils	connaissent	connaîtront	connaissaient	connurent
coudre	je	couds	coudrai	cousais	cousis
to sew	tu	couds	coudras	cousais	cousis
cousant	il	coud	coudra	cousait	cousit
cousu	nous	cousons	coudrons	cousions	cousîmes
	vous	cousez	coudrez	cousiez	cousîtes
	ils	cousent	coudront	cousaient	cousirent
courir	je	cours	courrai	courais	courus
to run	tu	cours	courras	courais	courus
courant	il	court	courra	courait	courut
couru	nous	courons	courrons	courions	courûmes
	vous	courez	courrez	couriez	courûtes
	ils	courent	courront	couraient	coururent
craindre	je	crains	craindrai	craignais	craignis
to fear	tu	crains	craindras	craignais	craignis
craignant	il	craint	craindra	craignait	craignit
craint	nous	craignons	craindrons	craignions	craignîmes
	vous	craignez	craindrez	craigniez	craignîtes
	ils	craignent	craindront	craignaient	craignirent
croire	je	crois	croirai	croyais	crus
to believe	tu	crois	croiras	croyais	crus
croyant	il	croit	croira	croyait	crut
cru	nous	croyons	croirons	croyions	crûmes
	vous	croyez	croirez	croyiez	crûtes
	ils	croient	croiront	croyaient	crurent

CONDITIONNEL	IMPÉRATIF	SUBJONCTIF	
		PRÉSENT	IMPARFAIT
conduirais		conduise	conduisisse
conduirais	conduis	conduises	conduisisses
conduirait		conduise	conduisît
conduirions	conduisons	conduisions	conduisissions
conduiriez	conduisez	conduisiez	conduisissiez
conduiraient		conduisent	conduisissent
connaîtrais		connaisse	connusse
connaîtrais	connais	connaisses	connusses
connaîtrait		connaisse	connût
connaîtrions	connaissons	connaissions	connussions
connaîtriez	connaissez	connaissiez	connussiez
connaîtraient		connaissent	connussent
coudrais		couse	cousisse
coudrais	couds	couses	cousisses
coudrait		couse	cousît
coudrions	cousons	cousions	cousissions
coudriez	cousez	cousiez	cousissiez
coudraient		cousent	cousissent
courrais		coure	courusse
courrais	cours	coures	courusses
courrait		coure	courût
courrions	courons	courions	courussions
courriez	courez	couriez	courussiez
courraient		courent	courussent
craindrais		craigne	craignisse
craindrais	crains	craignes	craignisses
craindrait		craigne	craignît
craindrions	craignons	craignions	craignissions
craindriez	craignez	craigniez	craignissiez
craindraient		craignent	craignissent
croirais		croie	crusse
croirais	crois	croies	crusses
croirait		croie	crût
croirions	croyons	croyions	crussions
croiriez	croyez	croyiez	crussiez
croiraient		croient	crussent

INFINITIF		INDICATIF			
PARTICIPES		PRÉSENT	FUTUR	IMPARFAIT	PASSÉ SIMPLE
croître	je	croîs	croîtrai	croissais	crûs
to grow	tu	croîs	croîtras	croissais	crûs
croissant	il	croît	croîtra	croissait	crût
crû	nous	croissons	croîtrons	croissions	crûmes
	vous	croissez	croîtrez	croissiez	crûtes
	ils	croissent	croîtront	croissaient	crûrent
cueillir	je	cueille	cueillerai	cueillais	cueillis
to gather	tu	cueilles	cueilleras	cueillais	cueillis
to pick	il	cueille	cueillera	cueillait	cueillit
cueillant	nous	cueillons	cueillerons	cueillions	cueillîmes
cueilli	vous	cueillez	cueillerez	cueilliez	cueillîtes
	ils	cueillent	cueilleront	cueillaient	cueillirent
devoir	je	dois	devrai	devais	dus
to owe, must	tu	dois	devras	devais	dus
devant	il	doit	devra	devait	dut
dû, due	nous	devons	devrons	devions	dûmes
	vous	devez	devrez	deviez	dûtes
	ils	doivent	devront	devaient	durent
dire	je	dis	dirai	disais	dis
to say	tu	dis	diras	disais	dis
disant	il	dit	dira	disait	dit
dit	nous	disons	dirons	disions	dîmes
	vous	dites	direz	disiez	dîtes
	ils	disent	diront	disaient	dirent
dormir	je	dors	dormirai	dormais	dormis
to sleep	tu	dors	dormiras	dormais	dormis
dormant	il	dort	dormira	dormait	dormit
dormi	nous	dormons	dormirons	dormions	dormimes
	vous	dormez	dormirez	dormiez	dormîtes
	ils	dorment	dormiront	dormaient	dormirent
écrire	j'	écris	écrirai	écrivais	écrivis
to write	tu	écris	écriras	écrivais	écrivis
écrivant	il	écrit	écrira	écrivait	écrivit
écrit	nous	écrivons	écrirons	écrivions	écrivîmes
	vous	écrivez	écrirez	écriviez	écrivîtes
	ils	écrivent	écriront	écrivaient	écrivirent

CONDITIONNEL	IMPÉRATIF	SUBJONCTIF	
		PRÉSENT	IMPARFAIT
croîtrais		croisse	crûsse
croîtrais	croîs	croisses	crûsses
croîtrait		croisse	crût
croîtrions	croissons	croissions	crûssions
croîtriez	croissez	croissiez	crûssiez
croîtraient		croissent	crûssent
cueillerais		cueille	cueillisse
cueillerais	cueille	cueilles	cueillisses
cueillerait		cueille	cueillît
cueillerions	cueillons	cueillions	cueillissions
cueilleriez	cueillez	cueilliez	cueillissiez
cueilleraient		cueillent	cueillissent
devrais		doive	dusse
devrais	dois	doives	dusses
devrait		doive	dût
devrions	devons	devions	dussions
devriez	devez	deviez	dussiez
devraient		doivent	dussent
dirais		dise	disse
dirais	dis	dises	disses
dirait		dise	dît
dirions	disons	disions	dissions
diriez	dites	disiez	dissiez
diraient		disent	dissent
dormirais		dorme	dormisse
dormirais	dors	dormes	dormisses
dormirait		dorme	dormît
dormirions	dormons	dormions	dormissions
dormiriez	dormez	dormiez	dormissez
dormiraient		dorment	dormissent
écrirais		écrive	écrivisse
écrirais	écris	écrives	écrivisses
écrirait		écrive	écrivît
écririons	écrivons	écrivions	écrivissions
écririez	écrivez	écriviez	écrivissiez
écriraient		écrivent	écrivissent

| INFINITIF | | INDICATIF | | | |
PARTICIPES		PRÉSENT	FUTUR	IMPARFAIT	PASSÉ SIMPLE
envoyer	j'	envoie	enverrai	envoyais	envoyai
to send	tu	envoies	enverras	envoyais	envoyas
envoyant	il	envoie	enverra	envoyait	envoya
envoyé	nous	envoyons	enverrons	envoyions	envoyâmes
	vous	envoyez	enverrez	envoyiez	envoyâtes
	ils	envoient	enverront	envoyaient	envoyèrent
faire	je	fais	ferai	faisais	fis
to do	tu	fais	feras	faisais	fis
to make	il	fait	fera	faisait	fit
faisant	nous	faisons	ferons	faisions	fîmes
fait	vous	faites	ferez	faisiez	fîtes
	ils	font	feront	faisaient	firent
falloir	il	faut	faudra	fallait	fallut

to be necessary, must
No present participle
Past participle: fallu

This is an impersonal verb conjugated in the third person singular only.

fuir	je	fuis	fuirai	fuyais	fuis
to flee	tu	fuis	fuiras	fuyais	fuis
fuyant	il	fuit	fuira	fuyait	fuit
fui	nous	fuyons	fuirons	fuyions	fuîmes
	vous	fuyez	fuirez	fuyiez	fuîtes
	ils	fuient	fuiront	fuyaient	fuirent
haïr	je	hais	haïrai	haïssais	haïs
to hate	tu	hais	haïras	haïssais	haïs
haïssant	il	hait	haïra	haïssait	haït
haï	nous	haïssons	haïrons	haïssions	haïmes
	vous	haïssez	haïrez	haïssiez	haïtes
	ils	haïssent	haïront	haïssaient	haïrent
lire	je	lis	lirai	lisais	lus
to read	tu	lis	liras	lisais	lus
lisant	il	lit	lira	lisait	lut
lu	nous	lisons	lirons	lisions	lûmes
	vous	lisez	lirez	lisiez	lûtes
	ils	lisent	liront	lisaient	lurent

CONDITIONNEL	IMPÉRATIF	SUBJONCTIF	
		PRÉSENT	IMPARFAIT
enverrais		envoie	envoyasse
enverrais	envoie	envoies	envoyasses
enverrait		envoie	envoyât
enverrions	envoyons	envoyions	envoyassions
enverriez	envoyez	envoyiez	envoyassiez
enverraient		envoyent	envoyassent
ferais		fasse	fisse
ferais	fais	fasses	fisses
ferait		fasse	fît
ferions	faisons	fassions	fissions
feriez	faites	fassiez	fissiez
feraient		fassent	fissent
faudrait		faille	fallût
fuirais		fuie	fuisse
fuirais	fuis	fuies	fuisses
fuirait		fuie	fuît
fuirions	fuyons	fuyions	fuissions
fuiriez	fuyez	fuyiez	fuissiez
fuiraient		fuient	fuissent
haïrais		haïsse	haïsse
haïrais	hais	haïsses	haïsses
haïrait		haïsse	haït
haïrions	haïssons	haïssions	haïssions
haïriez	haïssez	haïssiez	haïssiez
haïraient		haïssent	haïssent
lirais		lise	lusse
lirais	lis	lises	lusses
lirait		lise	lusse
lirions	lisons	lisions	lussions
liriez	lisez	lisiez	lussiez
liraient		lisent	lussent

INFINITIF		INDICATIF			
PARTICIPES		PRÉSENT	FUTUR	IMPARFAIT	PASSÉ SIMPLE
mettre	je	mets	mettrai	mettais	mis
to put	tu	mets	mettras	mettais	mis
mettant	il	met	mettra	mettait	mit
mis	nous	mettons	mettrons	mettions	mîmes
	vous	mettez	mettrez	mettiez	mîtes
	ils	mettent	mettront	mettaient	mirent
moudre	je	mouds	moudrai	moulais	moulus
to grind	tu	mouds	moudras	moulais	moulus
moulant	il	moud	moudra	moulait	moulut
moulu	nous	moulons	moudrons	moulions	moulûmes
	vous	moulez	moudrez	mouliez	moulûtes
	ils	moulent	moudront	moulaient	moulurent
mourir	je	meurs	mourrai	mourais	mourus
to die	tu	meurs	mourras	mourais	mourus
mourant	il	meurt	mourra	mourait	mourut
mort	nous	mourons	mourrons	mourions	mourûmes
	vous	mourez	mourrez	mouriez	mourûtes
	ils	meurent	mourront	mouraient	moururent
mouvoir	je	meus	mouvrai	mouvais	mus
to move	tu	meus	mouvras	mouvais	mus
mouvant	il	meut	mouvra	mouvait	mut
mû, mue	nous	mouvons	mouvrons	mouvions	mûmes
	vous	mouvez	mouvrez	mouviez	mûtes
	ils	meuvent	mouvront	mouvaient	murent
naître	je	nais	naîtrai	naissais	naquis
to be born	tu	nais	naîtras	naissais	naquis
naissant	il	naît	naîtra	naissait	naquit
né	nous	naissons	naîtrons	naissions	naquîmes
	vous	naissez	naîtrez	naissiez	naquîtes
	ils	naissent	naîtront	naissaient	naquirent
ouvrir	j'	ouvre	ouvrirai	ouvrais	ouvris
to open	tu	ouvres	ouvriras	ouvrais	ouvris
ouvrant	il	ouvre	ouvrira	ouvrait	ouvrit
ouvert	nous	ouvrons	ouvrirons	ouvrions	ouvrîmes
	vous	ouvrez	ouvrirez	ouvriez	ouvrîtes
	ils	ouvrent	ouvriront	ouvraient	ouvrirent

CONDITIONNEL	IMPÉRATIF	SUBJONCTIF	
		PRÉSENT	IMPARFAIT
mettrais		mette	misse
mettrais	mets	mettes	misses
mettrait		mette	mît
mettrions	mettons	mettions	missions
mettriez	mettez	mettiez	missiez
mettraient		mettent	missent
moudrais		moule	moulusse
moudrais	mouds	moules	moulusses
moudrait		moule	moulût
moudrions	moulons	moulions	moulussions
moudriez	moulez	mouliez	moulussiez
moudraient		moulent	moulussent
mourrais		meure	mourusse
mourrais	meurs	meures	mourusses
mourrait		meure	mourût
mourrions	mourons	mourions	mourussions
mourriez	mourez	mouriez	mourussiez
mourraient		meurent	mourussent
mouvrais		meuve	musse
mouvrais	meus	meuves	musses
mouvrait		meuve	musse
mouvrions	mouvons	mouvions	mussions
mouvriez	mouvez	mouviez	mussiez
mouvraient		meuvent	mussent
naîtrais		naisse	naquisse
naîtrais	nais	naisses	naquisses
naîtrait		naisse	naquît
naîtrions	naissons	naissions	naquissions
naîtriez	naissez	naissiez	naquissiez
naîtraient		naissent	naquissent
ouvrirais		ouvre	ouvrisse
ouvrirais	ouvre	ouvres	ouvrisses
ouvrirait		ouvre	ouvrît
ouvririons	ouvrons	ouvrions	ouvrissions
ouvririez	ouvrez	ouvriez	ouvrissiez
ouvriraient		ouvrent	ouvrissent

INFINITIF PARTICIPES		INDICATIF			
		PRESENT	FUTUR	IMPARFAIT	PASSÉ SIMPLE
partir	je	pars	partirai	partais	partis
to leave	tu	pars	partiras	partais	partis
to go away	il	part	partira	partait	partit
partant	nous	partons	partirons	partions	partîmes
parti	vous	partez	partirez	partiez	partîtes
	ils	partent	partiront	partaient	partirent
peindre	je	peins	peindrai	peignais	peignis
to paint	tu	peins	peindras	peignais	peignis
peignant	il	peint	peindra	peignait	peignit
peint	nous	peignons	peindrons	peignions	peignîmes
	vous	peignez	peindrez	peigniez	peignîtes
	ils	peignent	peindront	peignaient	peignirent
plaire	je	plais	plairai	plaisais	plus
to please	tu	plais	plairas	plaisais	plus
plaisant	il	plaît	plaira	plaisait	plut
plu	nous	plaisons	plairons	plaisions	plûmes
	vous	plaisez	plairez	plaisiez	plûtes
	ils	plaisent	plairont	plaisaient	plurent
pleuvoir	il	pleut	pleuvra	pleuvait	plut
to rain					
pleuvant					
plu					

This is an impersonal verb.

pourvoir	je	pourvois	pourvoirai	pourvoyais	pourvus
to provide	tu	pourvois	pourvoiras	pourvoyais	pourvus
pourvoyant	il	pouvoit	pourvoira	pourvoyait	pourvut
pourvu	nous	pourvoyons	pourvoirons	pourvoyions	pourvûmes
	vous	pourvoyez	pourvoirez	pourvoyiez	pourvûtes
	ils	pourvoient	pourvoiront	pourvoyaient	pourvurent
pouvoir	je	peux, puis	pourrai	pouvais	pus
to be able	tu	peux	pourras	pouvais	pus
can	il	peut	pourra	pouvait	put
pouvant	nous	pouvons	pourrons	pouvions	pûmes
pu	vous	pouvez	pourrez	pouviez	pûtes
	ils	peuvent	pourront	pouvaient	purent

CONDITIONNEL	IMPÉRATIF	SUBJONCTIF	
		PRÉSENT	IMPARFAIT
partirais		parte	partisse
partirais	pars	partes	partisses
partirait		parte	partît
partirions	partons	partions	partissions
partiriez	partez	partiez	partissiez
partiraient		partent	partissent
peindrais		peigne	peignisse
peindrais	peins	peignes	peignisses
peindrait		peigne	peignisse
peindrions	peignons	peignions	peignissions
peindriez	peignez	peigniez	peignissiez
peindraient		peignent	peignissent
plairais		plaise	plusse
plairais	plais	plaises	plusses
plairait		plaise	plût
plairions	plaisons	plaisions	plussions
plairiez	plaisez	plaisiez	plussiez
plairaient		plaisent	plussent
pleuvrait		pleuve	plût
pourvoirais		pourvoie	pourvusse
pourvoirais	pourvois	pourvoies	pourvusses
pourvoirait		pourvoie	pourvût
pourvoirions	pourvoyons	pourvoyions	pourvussions
pourvoiriez	pourvoyez	pourvoyiez	pourvussiez
pourvoiraient		pourvoient	pourvussent
pourrais		puisse	pusse
pourrais		puisses	pusses
pourrait		puisse	pût
pourrions		puissions	pussions
pourriez		puissiez	pussiez
pourraient		puissent	pussent

INFINITIF		INDICATIF			
PARTICIPES		PRÉSENT	FUTUR	IMPARFAIT	PASSÉ SIMPLE
prendre	je	prends	prendrai	prenais	pris
to take	tu	prends	prendras	prenais	pris
prenant	il	prend	prendra	prenait	prit
pris	nous	prenons	prendrons	prenions	prîmes
	vous	prenez	prendrez	preniez	prîtes
	ils	prennent	prendront	prenaient	prirent
recevoir	je	reçois	recevrai	recevais	reçus
to receive	tu	reçois	recevras	recevais	reçus
recevant	il	reçoit	recevra	recevait	reçut
reçu	nous	recevons	recevrons	recevions	reçûmes
	vous	recevez	recevrez	receviez	reçûtes
	ils	reçoivent	recevront	recevaient	reçurent
résoudre	je	résous	résoudrai	résolvais	résolus
to resolve	tu	résous	résoudras	résolvais	résolus
résolvant	il	résout	résoudra	résolvait	résolut
résolu	nous	résolvons	résoudrons	résolvions	résolûmes
	vous	résolvez	résoudrez	résolviez	résolûtes
	ils	résolvent	résoudront	résolvaient	résolurent
rire	je	ris	rirai	riais	ris
to laugh	tu	ris	riras	riais	ris
riant	il	rit	rira	riait	rit
ri	nous	rions	rirons	riions	rîmes
	vous	riez	rirez	riiez	rîtes
	ils	rient	riront	riaient	rirent
savoir	je	sais	saurai	savais	sus
to know	tu	sais	sauras	savais	sus
sachant	il	sait	saura	savait	sut
su	nous	savons	saurons	savions	sûmes
	vous	savez	saurez	saviez	sûtes
	ils	savent	sauront	savaient	surent
servir	je	sers	servirai	servais	servis
to serve	tu	sers	serviras	servais	servis
servant	il	sert	servira	servait	servit
servi	nous	servons	servirons	servions	servîmes
	vous	servez	servirez	serviez	servîtes
	ils	servent	serviront	servaient	servirent

CONDITIONNEL	IMPÉRATIF	SUBJONCTIF	
		PRÉSENT	IMPARFAIT
prendrais		prenne	prisse
prendrais	prends	prennes	prisses
prendrait		prenne	prît
prendrions	prenons	prenions	prissions
prendriez	prenez	preniez	prissiez
prendraient		prennent	prissent
recevrais		reçoive	reçusse
recevrais	reçois	reçoives	reçusses
recevrait		reçoive	reçût
recevrions	recevons	recevions	reçussions
recevriez	recevez	receviez	reçussiez
recevraient		reçoivent	reçussent
résoudrais		résolve	résolusse
résoudrais	résous	résolves	résolusses
résoudrait		résolve	résolût
résoudrions	résolvons	résolvions	résolussions
résoudriez	résolvez	résolviez	résolussiez
résoudraient		résolvent	résolussent
rirais		rie	risse
rirais	ris	ries	risses
rirait		rie	rît
ririons	rions	riions	rissions
ririez	riez	riiez	rissiez
riraient		rient	rissent
saurais		sache	susse
saurais	sache	saches	susses
saurait		sache	sût
saurions	sachons	sachions	sussions
sauriez	sachez	sachiez	sussiez
sauraient		sachent	sussent
servirais		serve	servisse
servirais	sers	serves	servisses
servirait		serve	servît
servirions	servons	servions	servissions
serviriez	servez	serviez	servissiez
serviraient		servent	servissent

INFINITIF PARTICIPES		PRÉSENT	FUTUR	IMPARFAIT	PASSÉ SIMPLE
suffire *to suffice* suffisant suffi	je tu il nous vous ils	suffis suffis suffit suffisons suffisez suffisent	suffirai suffiras suffira suffirons suffirez suffiront	suffisais suffisais suffisait suffisions suffisiez suffisaient	suffis suffis suffit suffîmes suffîtes suffirent
suivre *to follow* suivant suivi	je tu il nous vous ils	suis suis suit suivons suivez suivent	suivrai suivras suivra suivrons suivrez suivront	suivais suivais suivait suivions suiviez suivaient	suivis suivis suivit suivîmes suivîtes suivirent
tenir *to hold* tenant tenu	je tu il nous vous ils	tiens tiens tient tenons tenez tiennent	tiendrai tiendras tiendra tiendrons tiendrez tiendront	tenais tenais tenait tenions teniez tenaient	tins tins tint tînmes tîntes tinrent
traire *to milk* trayant trait	je tu il nous vous ils	trais trais trait trayons trayez traient	trairai trairas traira trairons trairez trairont	trayais trayais trayait trayions trayiez trayaient	
vaincre *to conquer* *to vanquish* vainquant vaincu	je tu il nous vous ils	vaincs vaincs vainc vainquons vainquez vainquent	vaincrai vaincras vaincra vaincrons vaincrez vaincront	vainquais vainquais vainquait vainquions vainquiez vainquaient	vainquis vainquis vainquit vainquîmes vainquîtes vainquirent
valoir *to be worth* valant valu	je tu il nous vous ils	vaux vaux vaut valons valez valent	vaudrai vaudras vaudra vaudrons vaudrez vaudront	valais valais valait valions valiez valaient	valus valus valut valûmes valûtes valurent

CONDITIONNEL	IMPÉRATIF	SUBJONCTIF	
		PRÉSENT	IMPARFAIT
suffirais		suffise	suffisse
suffirais	suffis	suffises	suffisses
suffirait		suffise	suffît
suffirions	suffisons	suffisions	suffissions
suffiriez	suffisez	suffisiez	suffissiez
suffiraient		suffisent	suffissent
suivrais		suive	suivisse
suivrais	suis	suives	suivisses
suivrait		suive	suivît
suivrions	suivons	suivions	suivissions
suivriez	suivez	suiviez	suivissiez
suivraient		suivent	suivissent
tiendrais		tienne	tinsse
tiendrais	tiens	tiennes	tinsses
tiendrait		tienne	tînt
tiendrions	tenons	tenions	tinssions
tiendriez	tenez	teniez	tinssiez
tiendraient		tiennent	tinssent
trairais		traie	
trairais	trais	traies	
trairait		traie	
trairions	trayons	trayions	
trairiez	trayez	trayiez	
trairaient		traient	
vaincrais		vainque	vainquisse
vaincrais	vaincs	vainques	vainquisses
vaincrait		vainque	vainquît
vaincrions	vainquons	vainquions	vainquissions
vaincriez	vainquez	vainquiez	vainquissiez
vaincraient		vainquent	vainquissent
vaudrais		vaille	valusse
vaudrais	vaux	vailles	valusses
vaudrait		vaille	valût
vaudrions	valons	valions	valussions
vaudriez	valez	valiez	valussiez
vaudraient		vaillent	valussent

INFINITIF		INDICATIF			
PARTICIPES		PRÉSENT	FUTUR	IMPARFAIT	PASSÉ SIMPLE
venir	je	viens	viendrai	venais	vins
to come	tu	viens	viendras	venais	vins
venant	il	vient	viendra	venait	vint
venu	nous	venons	viendrons	venions	vînmes
	vous	venez	viendrez	veniez	vîntes
	ils	viennent	viendront	venaient	vinrent
vêtir	je	vêts	vêtirai	vêtais	vêtis
to dress	tu	vêts	vêtiras	vêtais	vêtis
to clothe	il	vêt	vêtira	vêtait	vêtit
vêtant	nous	vêtons	vêtirons	vêtions	vêtîmes
vêtu	vous	vêtez	vêtirez	vêtiez	vêtîtes
	ils	vêtent	vêtiront	vêtaient	vêtirent
vivre	je	vis	vivrai	vivais	vécus
to live	tu	vis	vivras	vivais	vécus
vivant	il	vit	vivra	vivait	vécut
vécu	nous	vivons	vivrons	vivions	vécûmes
	vous	vivez	vivrez	viviez	vécûtes
	ils	vivent	vivront	vivaient	vécurent
voir	je	vois	verrai	voyais	vis
to see	tu	vois	verras	voyais	vis
voyant	il	voit	verra	voyait	vit
vu	nous	voyons	verrons	voyions	vîmes
	vous	voyez	verrez	voyiez	vîtes
	ils	voient	verront	voyaient	virent
vouloir	je	veux	voudrai	voulais	voulus
to want	tu	veux	voudras	voulais	voulus
to wish	il	veut	voudra	voulait	voulut
voulant	nous	voulons	voudrons	voulions	voulûmes
voulu	vous	voulez	voudrez	vouliez	voulûtes
	ils	veulent	voudront	voulaient	voulurent

CONDITIONNEL	IMPÉRATIF	SUBJONCTIF	
		PRÉSENT	IMPARFAIT
viendrais		vienne	vinsse
viendrais	viens	viennes	vinsses
viendrait		vienne	vînt
viendrions	venons	venions	vinssions
viendriez	venez	veniez	vinssiez
viendraient		viennent	vinssent
vêtirais		vête	vêtisse
vêtirais	vêts	vêtes	vêtisses
vêtirait		vête	vêtît
vêtirions	vêtons	vêtions	vêtissions
vêtiriez	vêtez	vêtiez	vêtissiez
vêtiraient		vêtent	vêtissent
vivrais		vive	vécusse
vivrais	vis	vives	vécusses
vivrait		vive	vécût
vivrions	vivons	vivions	vécussions
vivriez	vivez	viviez	vécussiez
vivraient		vivent	vécussent
verrais		voie	visse
verrais	vois	voies	visses
verrait		voie	vît
verrions	voyons	voyions	vissions
verriez	voyez	voyiez	vissiez
verraient		voient	vissent
voudrais		veuille	voulusse
voudrais	veux (veuille)	veuilles	voulusses
voudrait		veuille	voulût
voudrions	voulons	voulions	voulussions
voudriez	voulez	vouliez	voulussiez
voudraient		veuillent	voulussent

59

List of the most common irregular verbs (third group)

INFINITIVE	VERB TYPE	INFINITIVE	VERB TYPE
abattre	battre	convenir	venir
abstenir(s')	tenir	correspondre	vendre
abstraire	traire	corrompre	vendre
accourir	courir	couvrir	ouvrir
accroître	croître	cuire	conduire
accueillir	cueillir	débattre	battre
adjoindre	craindre	décevoir	recevoir
admettre	mettre	découdre	coudre
advenir	venir	découvrir	couvrir
apercevoir	recevoir	décrire	écrire
apparaître	connaître	décroître	croître
appartenir	tenir	déduire	conduire
apprendre	prendre	défaillir	assaillir
astreindre	peindre	défaire	faire
atteindre	vendre	défendre	vendre
ceindre	peindre	démentir	partir
circonscrire	écrire	démettre	mettre
circonvenir	venir	démordre	vendre
combattre	battre	dépeindre	peindre
commettre	mettre	dépendre	vendre
comparaître	connaître	déplaire	plaire
complaire	plaire	dépourvoir	pourvoir
comprendre	prendre	déprendre	prendre
compromettre	mettre	désapprendre	prendre
concevoir	recevoir	descendre	vendre
concourir	courir	desservir	servir
condescendre	vendre	déteindre	peindre
confondre	vendre	détendre	vendre
conquérir	acquérir	détenir	tenir
consentir	partir	détruire	conduire
construire	conduire	devenir	venir
contenir	tenir	dévêtir	vêtir
contraindre	peindre	discourir	courir
contredire	dire	disjoindre	craindre
contrefaire	faire	disparaître	connaître
convaincre	vaincre	dissoudre	absoudre

[164]

INFINITIVE	VERB TYPE	INFINITIVE	VERB TYPE
distraire	traire	nuire (p.p. nui)	conduire
ébattre(s')	battre	obtenir	tenir
éconduire	conduire	offrir	ouvrir
élire	lire	omettre	mettre
émettre	mettre	paraître	connaître
émouvoir	mouvoir	parcourir	courir
encourir	courir	parfaire	faire
endormir	dormir	parvenir	venir
enduire	conduire	pendre	vendre
enfreindre	peindre	percevoir	recevoir
enfuir(s')	fuir	perdre	vendre
enquérir(s')	acquérir	permettre	mettre
entendre	vendre	plaindre	craindre
entremettre	mettre	pondre	vendre
entreprendre	prendre	poursuivre	suivre
entretenir	tenir	prédire	dire
entrevoir	voir	prescrire	écrire
entrouvrir	ouvrir	pressentir	partir
éprendre(s')	prendre	prétendre	vendre
équivaloir	valoir	prévenir	venir
éteindre	peindre	prévoir	voir
étendre	vendre	produire	conduire
exclure	conclure	promettre	mettre
extraire	traire	proscrire	écrire
feindre	peindre	provenir	venir
fendre	vendre	rabattre	battre
fondre	vendre	rasseoir	asseoir
frire	suffire	réadmettre	mettre
geindre	peindre	réapparaître	connaître
inclure	conclure	réapprendre	prendre
induire	conduire	reconduire	conduire
inscrire	écrire	reconnaître	connaître
instruire	conduire	reconstruire	conduire
interdire	dire	recourir	courir
interrompre	vendre	recouvrir	ouvrir
intervenir	venir	récrire	écrire
introduire	conduire	recueillir	cueillir
joindre	craindre	redescendre	vendre
luire	conduire	redevenir	venir
maintenir	tenir	redire	dire
malfaire	faire	réduire	conduire
méconnaître	connaître	refaire	faire
médire	dire	réinscrire	écrire
méprendre	prendre	réintroduire	conduire
mordre	vendre	rejoindre	craindre

INFINITIVE	VERB TYPE	INFINITIVE	VERB TYPE
relire	lire	sentir	partir
reluire	conduire	sortir	partir
remettre	mettre	souffrir	ouvrir
rendormir	dormir	soumettre	mettre
rendre	vendre	sourire	rire
répandre	vendre	souscrire	écrire
reparaître	connaître	sous-entendre	vendre
repartir	partir	soustraire	traire
repeindre	peindre	soutenir	tenir
rependre	vendre	souvenir (se)	venir
repentir (se)	partir	subvenir	venir
répondre	vendre	surfaire	faire
reprendre	prendre	surprendre	prendre
reproduire	conduire	survenir	venir
requérir	acquérir	survivre	vivre
résoudre	absoudre	suspendre	vendre
ressentir	partir	taire	plaire
ressouvenir (se)	venir	teindre	peindre
revendre	vendre	tendre	vendre
revenir	venir	tondre	vendre
revivre	vivre	tordre	vendre
revoir	voir	traduire	conduire
rompre	vendre	transcrire	écrire
rouvrir	ouvrir	transmettre	mettre
satisfaire	faire	transparaître	connaître
secourir	courir	tressaillir	assaillir
séduire	conduire		

Index

Numbers in heavy type refer to pages. References in parentheses refer to sections.